MULTICULTURAL EDUC.

James A. Banks, Seri

D0020785

We Can't Teach What We Don't Know

White Teachers, Multiracial Schools

SECOND EDITION

GARY R. HOWARD

Foreword by Sonia Nieto

Teachers College, Columbia University
New York and London

Published by Teachers College Press, 1234 Amsterdam Avenue, New York, NY 10027

Library of Congress Cataloging-in-Publication Data

Howard, Gary R.
    We can't teach what we don't know : white teachers, multiracial schools / Gary R. Howard ; foreword by Sonia Nieto.—2nd ed.
        p. cm. — (Multicultural education series)
    Includes bibliographical references and index.
    ISBN-13: 978-0-8077-4665-3 (pbk. : alk. paper)
    ISBN-10: 0-8077-4665-7 (pbk. : alk. paper)
        1. Discrimination in education—United States. 2. Multicultural education—United States. 3. Whites—Race identity. 4. Racism.
    I. Title. II. Multicultural education series (New York, N.Y.)
    LC212.2.H68 2006
    370.117—dc22   2005052986

ISBN-13: 978-0-8077-4665-3 (paper)   ISBN-10: 0-8077-4665-7 (paper)

Printed on acid-free paper
Manufactured in the United States of America

13 12 11 10 09 08 07 06   8 7 6 5 4 3 2 1

To James A. Banks,
for inspiring me with a vision worthy
of a lifetime of work.

To my grandchildren,
Orion, Mihna, and Chelan,
who are the future—may your teachers serve you well.

And once again to Lotus,
who is still the best teacher I have known.

Contents

Series Foreword

The nation's deepening ethnic texture, interracial tension and conflict, and the increasing percentage of students who speak a first language other than English make multicultural education imperative in the 21st century. The U.S. Census Bureau (2000) estimates that people of color made up 28% of the nation's population in 2000 and predicts that they will make up 38% in 2025 and 50% in 2050 (El Nasser, 2004).

American classrooms are experiencing the largest influx of immigrant students since the beginning of the 20th century. About a million immigrants are making the United States their home each year (Martin & Midgley, 1999). More than seven and one-half million legal immigrants settled in the United States between 1991 and 1998, most of whom came from nations in Latin America and Asia (Riche, 2000). A significant number also come from the West Indies and Africa. A large but undetermined number of undocumented immigrants also enter the United States each year. The influence of an increasingly ethnically diverse population on the nation's schools, colleges, and universities is and will continue to be enormous.

Forty percent of the students enrolled in the nation's schools in 2001 were students of color. This percentage is increasing each year, primarily because of the growth in the percentage of Latino students (Martinez & Curry, 1999). In some of the nation's largest cities and metropolitan areas, such as Chicago, Los Angeles, Washington, DC, New York, Seattle, and San Francisco, half or more of the public school students are students of color. During the 1998–1999 school year, students of color made up 63.1% of the student population in the public schools of California, the nation's most populous state (California State Department of Education, 2000).

Language and religious diversity is also increasing among the nation's student population. In 2000, about 20% of the school-age population spoke a language at home other than English (U.S. Census Bureau, 2000). Harvard professor Diana L. Eck (2001) calls the United States the "most religiously diverse nation on earth" (p. 4). Islam is now the fastest-growing religion in the United States. Most teachers now in the classroom and in teacher education programs are likely to have students from diverse ethnic, racial, language, and religious groups in their classrooms during their careers. This is true for both inner-city and suburban teachers.

An important goal of multicultural education is to improve race relations and to help all students acquire the knowledge, attitudes, and skills needed to participate in cross-cultural interactions and in personal, social, and civic action that will help make our nation more democratic and just. Multicultural education is consequently as important for middle-class White suburban students as it is for students of color who live in the inner city. Multicultural education fosters the public good and the overarching goals of the commonwealth.

The major purpose of the *Multicultural Education Series* is to provide preservice educators, practicing educators, graduate students, scholars, and policymakers with an interrelated and comprehensive set of books that summarizes and analyzes important research, theory, and practice related to the education of ethnic, racial, cultural, and language groups in the United States and the education of mainstream students about diversity. The books in the *Series* provide research, theoretical, and practical knowledge about the behaviors and learning characteristics of students of color, language minority students, and low-income students. They also provide knowledge about ways to improve academic achievement and race relations in educational settings.

The definition of multicultural education in the *Handbook of Research on Multicultural Education* (Banks & Banks, 2004) is used in the *Series*: Multicultural education is *"a field of study designed to increase educational equity for all students that incorporates, for this purpose, content, concepts, principles, theories, and paradigms from history, the social and behavioral sciences, and particularly from ethnic studies and women's studies"* (p. xii). In the *Series*, as in the *Handbook*, multicultural education is considered a "metadiscipline."

The dimensions of multicultural education, developed by Banks (2004b) and described in the *Handbook of Research on Multicultural Education*, provide the conceptual framework for the development of the books in the *Series*. They are: *content integration, the knowledge construction process, prejudice reduction, an equity pedagogy,* and *an empowering school culture and social structure*. To implement multicultural education effectively, teachers and administrators must attend to each of the five dimensions of multicultural education. They should use content from diverse groups when teaching concepts and skills, help students to understand how knowledge in the various disciplines is constructed, help students to develop positive intergroup attitudes and behaviors, and modify their teaching strategies so that students from different racial, cultural, language, and social-class groups will experience equal educational opportunities. The total environment and culture of the school must also be transformed so that students from diverse groups will experience equal status in the culture and life of the school.

Although the five dimensions of multicultural education are highly interrelated, each requires deliberate attention and focus. Each book in the *Series* focuses on one or more of the dimensions, although each book deals with all of them to some extent because of the highly interrelated characteristics of the dimensions.

World events since the publication of the first edition of this insightful and visionary book have accentuated why it is needed and timely. Worldwide immigration is increasing racial, ethnic, cultural, language, and religious diversity throughout the United States, as well in other Western nations such as the United Kingdom, France, Germany, and Australia (Banks, 2004a). The Western world is perplexed, exhausted, and fear-ridden as it attempts to envision and implement viable and creative strategies to respond effectively to the conflicts in the Middle East and Islamic suicide bombers (Barber, 2003). These events have resulted in bombings that have created a reign of terror throughout the world—including the attacks on the Pentagon and the World Trade Center on September 11, 2001; the bombings of four commuter trains in Madrid, Spain on March 11, 2004; the bombings in the London transportation system on July 7, 2005; and the bombing of a Red Sea resort at Sharm el-Sheikh in Egypt on July 23, 2005.

We are living in a dangerous, confused, and troubled world—a world that needs leaders, educators, and classroom teachers who can bridge impermeable cultural, ethnic, and religious borders, envision new possibilities, invent novel paradigms, and engage in personal transformation and visionary action. The concepts, paradigms, and projects that facilitated the rise and triumph of the West between the 16th and 20th centuries are ineffective in the recreated world of the 21st century. The world is undergoing a transformation—and in the words of Thomas L. Friedman (2005)—"the world is flat." In the flat world described by Friedman, scientific and technological workers educated in Asian nations such as India and China are competing successfully—and sometimes outperforming—scientific and technological workers educated at universities in the United States. The United States can no longer take its scientific and technological superiority for granted. American students educated in Seattle, New York City, and Washington, DC, must now be prepared to compete directly for jobs with students educated in India, Pakistan, and China. This is because technology allows U.S. firms to export many service jobs to other nations where they can be done as well or better by foreign workers and for a fraction of the cost.

Effective teachers in a diverse and flat world need an education that enables them to attain new knowledge, paradigms, and perspectives on the United States and the world. They should acquire the knowledge and skills that will enable them to examine the assumptions that undergird concepts such as "the Westward Movement" and "American Exceptionalism." Teachers should also be able to examine the gap between American ideals and realities, and to develop a commitment to act to help close it. However, as this astute and engaging book makes clear, knowledge is essential but not sufficient for teachers in a diverse and flat world. Teachers must also critically analyze their ideologies, journeys, dispositions, and engage in personal transformation. Since it was first published, I have used this book as one of two texts in a teacher education course. It deeply engages my students, causes them to reflect intensely on their lives as they relate to race, and helps them to develop personal commitments to make their classrooms, schools, and the world more just and humane.

The first edition of this book helped thousands of classroom teachers to think deeply about race in U.S. society and to engage in personal transformation and action. I am confident that this second edition will touch the future and inspire a new generation of teachers to make the world a better place. I am pleased to recommend the second edition of this insightful and inspiring book to all educators who are committed to increasing educational equality and social justice in a divided and troubled world.

James A. Banks
Series Editor

REFERENCES

Banks, J. A. (Ed.). (2004a). *Diversity and citizenship education: Global perspectives.* San Francisco: Jossey-Bass.

Banks, J. A. (2004b). Multicultural education: Historical development, dimensions, and practice. In J. A. Banks & C. A. M. Banks (Eds.), *Handbook of research on multicultural education* (2nd ed., pp. 3–29). San Francisco: Jossey-Bass.

Banks, J. A., & Banks, C. A. M. (Eds.). (2004). *Handbook of research on multicultural education* (2nd ed.). San Francisco: Jossey-Bass.

Barber, B. R. (2003). *Fear's empire: War, terrorism, and democracy.* New York: Norton.

California State Department of Education. (2000). Available online at http://data1.cde.ca.gov/dataquest

Eck, D. L. (2001). *A new religious America: How a "Christian country" has become the world's most religiously diverse nation.* New York: HarperSanFrancisco.

Friedman, T. L. (2005). *The world is flat: A brief history of the twenty-first century.* New York: Farrar, Strauss & Giroux.

El Nasser, H. (2004, March 18). Census projects growing diversity: By 2050: Population burst, societal shifts. *USA Today,* p. 1A.

Martin, P., & Midgley, E. (1999). Immigration to the United States. *Population Bulletin, 54*(2), 1–44. Washington, DC: Population Reference Bureau.

Martinez, G. M., & Curry, A. E. (1999, September). *Current population reports: School enrollment—social and economic characteristics of students* [update]. Washington, DC: U.S. Census Bureau.

Riche, M. F. (2000). America's diversity and growth: Signposts for the 21st century. *Population Bulletin, 55*(2), 1–43. Washington, DC: Population Reference Bureau.

U. S. Census Bureau (2000). *Statistical abstract of the United States* (120th edition). Washington, DC: U.S. Government Printing Office.

Foreword

It was over a dozen years ago that I first read Gary Howard's article, "Whites in Multicultural Education: Rethinking Our Role" (1993), an article that was later to become the basis of his book, *We Can't Teach What We Don't Know: White Teachers, Multiracial Schools*. It was the first time I had read something that seriously challenged the widespread perception that Whites need not be concerned about multicultural education. I had always thought it odd that White teachers—who are after all the teachers of most students of color in U.S. schools—were largely missing from the discourse on multicultural education. In fact, I thought it was *particularly* crucial for White teachers to reflect on what it means to be teachers of African American, Latino, Asian, and American Indian students. I also thought it was important for White teachers to consider what it means to be *both* White and multicultural and *both* White and anti-racist. I had been waiting for years for an acknowledgment that Whites, too, need to engage in the difficult dialogue and action of multicultural education without, as Gary Howard writes in this book, having to "rip off their White skin."

Part of the process of including Whites in multicultural education means defining Whites as "ethnics" who have their own histories and identities. Without a recognition that Whites are ethnic—a designation usually reserved for anybody who is not White, and sometimes for those groups of European heritage that have not quite "melted" into the pot—it is too easy to characterize Whites as "normal" and others as "different" or "exotic." At the same time that I thought White identity needed to be included as a dimension of multicultural education, I also felt that this recognition needed to be accompanied by a critical and truthful acknowledgment of White privilege, power, and abuses throughout U.S. history. Especially important in this regard is for White teachers to recognize their complicity in creating and supporting the conditions in schools that lead to failure for so many students of color. Without this critical stance, White identity could become just another celebration, another example of the superficial rendering of multicultural education as "Heroes and Holidays" that happens in far too many schools.

Taking on an identity based on privilege and the oppression of others is difficult because it brings with it a great deal of inner turmoil and anguish. Many Whites, even those committed to diversity, prefer other routes. These include identifying with another culture or immersing themselves in work with people of color while avoiding direct work with other Whites. But as Howard points out as he chronicles the process of developing a healthy White identity, avoiding a painful reckoning with privilege and power does little to resolve the conundrum of how Whites can identify with their culture and heritage if these are understood as *only* negative and *only* oppressive. What is needed in the process of developing a healthy White identity is neither a narcissistic preoccupation with Whiteness nor a guilt-ridden journey that results only in immobilization. What is needed, in a word, is hope. This book provides that hope.

Gary Howard speaks of his own transformation as a rebirth. In his work with many other White educators over the years, he has documented that, like a birth, the transformation of White teachers is defined by both pain and possibility. Coming to terms with one's identity is a formidable task. This is true for all people, but for Whites it is especially troublesome because admitting that they have benefited unfairly from their White skin is not only personally disturbing, but also challenges head-on the myths of meritocracy and fair play with which they have been raised. This is a necessary process that Whites must undertake if they are to join the multicultural dialogue in an honest way. Just as the identities of people of color include more than simply being victims, the identities of Whites are about more than being victimizers. Involving Whites in multicultural education therefore needs to resolve two seemingly contradictory aims: to confront in a brutally honest way White oppression, and to promote the development of a healthy identity that is at the same time anti-racist and multicultural.

In this book, Gary Howard has managed to accomplish both of these aims, and he has done so admirably and with a blend of humanity and critique that is unusual in many academic discussions about controversial issues. The theoretical work he has developed on White identity orientations is groundbreaking, noteworthy because it is not simply a static formula for explicating an exceedingly complex phenomenon. What was missing until now in many of the discussions concerning the role of White teachers in multicultural education was a recognition that, in the words of Gary Howard, "there is not one way of being White, but many." For White teachers who undergo the difficult course of facing the implications of their privilege, it means that there can be more than just pain and suffering at the end. For teachers of other backgrounds it means that they are not alone, that they can look forward to having colleagues and allies who are committed to anti-racist multicultural education for all students. And, of course, ultimately, it is the students in our classrooms who benefit most because they will have teachers who grapple on an ongoing basis with the difficult issues of privilege and racism—teachers who understand what it means to think about these issues deeply and who are committed to providing all their students with a rigorous, supportive, caring, and quality education.

In the second edition of this important book, Gary Howard brings his vision squarely into the context of the twenty-first century. In public education, it is a context characterized by rigid accountability and unforgiving high-stakes testing, of public disdain for teachers, of the desertion of the profession by vast numbers of teachers who feel disrespected and, in many cases, unprepared to teach students different from themselves, and increasingly—through the adoption of a discourse of despair that sees only "gaps" in children of color—of the abandonment of these young people and the schools they attend. Yet it is clear that the "gaps" are not so much in the children as in the schools' policies and practices and in bigoted ideas about intelligence and worthiness, ideas that die hard even in this day and age. Focusing on teachers and prospective teachers, then, is even more urgent today than it was in 1999 when *We Can't Teach What We Don't Know* was first published. More teachers need to read this book, more schools need to make sure it is in their libraries, and more schools of education need to include it in their reading lists. Needless to say, one book cannot change the world—but it can begin the process.

Sonia Nieto
University of Massachusetts at Amherst

Acknowledgments

This book contains many stories and accounts from four decades of work in the field of multicultural education and social justice. None of the lessons and insights that have grown from these experiences would have been possible without the care and trust of the many colleagues, students, friends, and family members who have touched me deeply over the years. I thank each of them for allowing me into their lives.

I give special thanks to all of the staff members who have worked at the REACH Center for Multicultural Education over the past 30 years, in particular, Colleen Almojuela, Karen Aurand, Diane Christiansen, David Koyama, and Bettie Sing Luke. They have supported, challenged, and inspired me in my work, and much of what they have given me is reflected in these pages.

I am deeply indebted to my research associates, Michelle Woodfork on the first edition, and Patricia McDonald on the second edition, for their contributions to both the quality and the enjoyment of the writing process.

To inform the writing of this book, I invited several colleagues from widely diverse racial, ethnic, and cultural backgrounds to write personal narratives regarding their own racial identity development and experiences with social dominance and Whiteness. I thank each of these individuals for sharing their insightful and heartfelt stories with me: Colleen Almojuela, Bob Connors, Margaretha Finefrock, Bob Gallagher, Tyrone Howard, David Koyama, Lotus Linton-Howard, Tom McKenna, Aileen Moreton-Robinson, Jessie Myles, Michele Soria, Be Stoney, and Liz Sweeney.

Finally, special thanks goes to Anissa Dixon of the Omaha Public Schools for her creative design of the Achievement Triangle figures that appear in Chapter 7.

Introduction

> I fundamentally believe that educating all children, even those who are poor and non-White, is an achievable goal, *if* we truly value all children. Of course, that is the real question: Does American society truly value all of its children?
> —Pedro Noguera, *City Schools and the American Dream*

Three grandchildren have come into my life since the first publication of this book in 1999, each of them bringing various combinations of multiracial, multicultural, and multi-religious identity into our family. The issues that galvanized my passion for equity and social justice during the final four decades of the 20th century have now been refocused and personally intensified by the arrival of these children, energizing me for more work in the new century we and they are now creating.

In addition to my personal deepening of engagement over the years, I also sense a renewed urgency in our nation for addressing the central theme of this book, namely, the necessity to prepare a predominantly White teaching force to work effectively with an increasingly diverse student population. Since the first edition of this book, I have been invited into hundreds of school districts to address what is often seen as a disconnection between White teachers and students of color in our nation's classrooms. Whether in urban settings, where a high percentage of racially diverse students has been the norm for many years, or in suburban and exurban districts, where educators are now experiencing rapid growth in student diversity, the issue is equally clear: we have much work to do in creating the kinds of schools that work well for children of color.

The federal No Child Left Behind legislation, which has also come on the scene since the first publication of this book, has added to the current climate of increased urgency. While there are many problems with this federal mandate, not the least of which being that the increased accountability comes with tragically insufficient funding (Mathis, 2003), the primary benefit is that schools are now forced to pay attention to those students who are *not* achieving, and to disaggregate their achievement data by race, as well as other dimensions of difference. In spite of this increased focus on the achievement of diverse students, however, the NCLB legislation places little or no emphasis on increasing the cultural competence of teachers to work effectively with children from diverse racial and cultural backgrounds (Gay, Dingus, & Jackson, 2003; National Collaborative on Diversity in the Teaching Force, 2004). Politicians may do all they want to increase testing and accountability requirements and consequences, but if we as a nation fail to raise the cultural competence of our teachers to work effectively with diverse students, then the entire reform effort becomes merely a hollow exercise in futility. The politics of accountability have certainly intensified, but deep engagement and financial investment in the authentic issues of pedagogical transformation are still missing. That deficit is the focus of this book.

Partly as a result of the NCLB legislation, but even more so because of the long-term persistence and insistence of parents and educators of color, we are now paying more attention to the race-based academic achievement gap in our nation's schools. The National Assessment of Educational Progress consistently reports that the average eighth grade student of color performs at the same level of academic proficiency as the average fourth grade White student (National Center for Educational Statistics, 2003). Likewise, NCES reports a four-year reading gap between African American high school students and their White counterparts.

Some teachers, politicians, and educational leaders, wishing to avoid or minimize issues of race, would prefer to attribute the achievement gap to socioeconomic differences alone. While it is true that poverty correlates highly with school failure (Barton, 2004), it has also been repeatedly demonstrated that race functions independently of economics, evidenced by the fact that even middle and upper-middle class students of color fall below their low income White and Asian peers on most measures of academic achievement (R. Ferguson, 2000; Jencks & Phillips, 1998; Noguera, 2003). Because school success is so highly correlated with success in life, this race-based disequilibrium in academic achievement has become one of the core social justice issues of our time.

My work in the multicultural and social justice arena began over 40 years ago when I became embroiled in the Civil Rights Movement of the 1960s. Since then my journey has led me into multicultural teaching, curriculum development, writing, training, school reform activism, and the creation of the REACH Center for Multicultural Education, an organization that has for the past 30 years published classroom materials and designed staff development programs that are used internationally.

I offer this book as a practitioner's account of being engaged for most of my personal and professional life with issues of race, social justice, and diversity in education. In my work I have been a fellow traveler among thousands of other teachers and activists from all racial and cultural groups throughout the world who are seeking to map new routes to social healing. The fact that I am White has colored my journey in a particular way, and it is from this perspective that I write.

The original motivation for writing this book was embodied in an encounter I had while working with teachers in a school district that was experiencing rapid demographic change. Over the course of five years, this school system had grown from a 10% Hispanic student population to over 40%. I had been invited to deliver the opening day address to the entire school staff. The intent was to help teachers deal with the multicultural implications of their changing school population, and to address the unavoidable evidence that their schools were not effectively serving the academic achievement needs of Hispanic students. Following my keynote, I spent considerable time working with the high school faculty to help them develop more inclusive teaching strategies. In the past, Hispanic students had attended only one of the district's two high schools, while the other, which was seen as more "elite," had remained primarily White. With the changing demographics, however, both schools were experiencing rapid growth in Hispanic population. After the workshop, a White teacher who had taught in the "good" high school for 20 years came up to me with a puzzled look on her face, and said, "What I want to know is why are they sending these kids to our school?" I asked, "You mean the Hispanic kids?" She nodded, and I said, "Hispanic kids are coming to 'your' high school because they live here; they are a part of your community." She walked away shaking her head, obviously disenchanted with my response. Evidenced by this teacher and others I have encountered in my travels, it must sadly be acknowledged in response to Noguera's query in the opening quote, there are still many educators in our nation's schools who do not value *all* of our children.

DIVERSITY IS NOT A CHOICE

"Why are they sending these kids to us?" Projected onto the larger educational scene, the answer to this question is simple: They live here. The growing presence of diversity in our public school population is the face of our future. While experiencing the largest influx of immigrant children since the turn of the last century (Banks, 2006), public schools are also dealing with more language and religious diversity than most teachers are trained to embrace effectively in their classrooms (Eck, 2001; Garcia, 2005).

Children of color and multicultural complexity, like the new grandbabies in my family, will continue to come in ever-increasing numbers into our nation's classrooms. In the United States the population of students of color reached 30% in 1990, 34% in 1994, 40% in 2002, and will continue to increase throughout the twenty-first century (Hodgkinson, 1991, 2001, 2002; National Center for Educational Statistics, 1996, 2003). At the same time, Whites represent 90% of public school teachers, a figure that will remain high or possibly grow in the next few decades (Gay, Dingus & Jackson, 2003; National Center for Educational Statistics, 2003; National Education Association, 2003). In addition, some 40% of schools in the U.S. have no teachers of color in their classrooms (National Collaborative, 2004). The picture is clear: For the foreseeable future, the vast majority of teachers will be White while the student population will grow increasingly diverse. The need for teacher preparation is obvious, particularly given the fact that most practicing and prospective White teachers are themselves the products of predominantly White neighborhoods and predominantly White colleges of teacher education (Nieto, 1996). And, unfortunately, the reversal of desegregation efforts that has occured since the early 1990s has resulted in the increasing re-segregation of our nation's schools and produced a growing educational apartheid that virtually assures that most future White teachers will continue to come from racially isolated White schools and communities (Hardy, 2004; Kozol, 2005; Orfield & Lee, 2004).

Thus, at the present time in American public education we are faced with three simultaneous statistical realities: (1) our teacher force is mostly White, (2) our student population is highly diverse and growing in children of color, and (3) children of color are precisely the students most at risk of being caught on the negative end of the achievement gap. These statistics beg the question: Is there a causal relationship between the over-representation of White teachers in our classrooms and the under-performance of children of color in our nation's schools?

Diversity is not a choice, but our responses to it certainly are. And to date, all indicators point to the fact that our responses have not been adequate to deal with the full range of issues presented by the complexities of teaching in a multicultural nation. As I conduct my workshops with teachers throughout the United States and Australia each year, I ask participants, "What evidence is there that we have not yet solved the problems of racism and inequality in our schools and society?" Their answers are many and varied: disproportionate academic outcomes for different racial groups, increasing incidents of racially motivated violence and hate-group activity, inequalities in educational funding, inadequate preparation of teachers to deal effectively with increasing diversity, curriculum that remains Eurocentric and monocultural, political manipulation of ethnic and racial fears and hostilities, and resistance from educators, school boards, and communities to face the realities of their changing populations. Jonathan Kozol (2005) speaks passionately and insightfully to these issues in his new book, *The Shame of the Nation: The Restoration of Apartheid Schooling in America*, the title itself speaking to the depth of the social justice challenges facing us in our schools today. I find that many of my White peers in education, and certainly most of those from other racial and cultural groups, are not unaware of the issues facing us. We are, however, almost universally frustrated and confused regarding the solutions. It is the intent of this book to provide possible pathways to those solutions, not the least of which is to assure that the disproportionate presence of White teachers in our nation's classrooms is not causally related to the disproportionate presence of children of color in the lower quartiles of academic achievement.

While being interviewed by a National Public Radio affiliate, I was asked, "Given all of the years that you and others have been working in multicultural education, and all the energy we have invested in civil rights initiatives over the past 50 years, why haven't we solved the problems of racism and inequality?" I was struck by both the simplicity and the profundity of this question. Why, indeed, do social justice and real change still remain so illusive?

In the face of a teacher population that is primarily White and culturally isolated, a student population that is increasingly diverse, and educational outcomes that reflect persistent inequalities across racial differences, this book is my attempt to search for a deeper understanding of the personal and social dynamics that have made the process of healing so difficult. My work with educators in many different settings has convinced me that we have neither gone far enough in our analysis of the issues nor deep enough in our design of possible responses. We have dealt with the "what" and the "how" of multicultural teaching and learning, but we have not adequately addressed the "why" and the "who." Too often as White educators we have seen the problems as "out there," and we have conceptualized our role as one of "helping minority students." Seldom have we helped White educators look deeply and critically at the necessary changes and growth we ourselves must achieve if we are to work effectively with the real issues of race, equity, and social justice.

THE INNER WORK OF MULTICULTURAL TEACHING

At the close of the 20th century, President Clinton called for a renewed national conversation on race. Many activities were engaged around this topic, and since that time school districts throughout the nation have invited educators, students, and parents into the process of racial dialogue. I wondered then, and continue to question now, whether mere "conversation" will be enough. We seem to be able to talk incessantly about race without achieving real change. As one of my African American colleagues said to me after being invited into such a process in his school, "I'm tired of all this talk about a dialogue on race. What I want is to see the day when people quit calling me a 'nigger.'"

As compelling as the need for an ongoing conversation on issues of race may be, my friend's comment suggests that talk alone may be inadequate to the task. I am convinced there is a prior and equally compelling need for White people, particularly White educators in the United States and other nations of the West, to look within ourselves and realign our deepest assumptions and perceptions regarding the racial marker that we carry, namely Whiteness. We need to understand the dynamics of past and present dominance, face how we have been shaped by myths of superiority, and begin to sort out our thoughts, emotions, and behaviors relative to race and other dimensions of human diversity.

It is essential in this inner work of multicultural growth that we listen carefully to the perceptions others have of us, particularly students, parents, and colleagues from other racial and cultural groups. They can help us see ourselves in a clearer and truer light. We cannot fully and fruitfully engage in meaningful dialogue across the differences of race and culture without doing the work of personal transformation. If we as White educators are not deeply moved and transformed, there is little hope that anything else will significantly shift. We must assume that we will be changed in the process of engagement and dialogue. We cannot help our students overcome the negative repercussions of past and present racial dominance if we have not unraveled the remnants of dominance that still lingers in our minds, hearts, and habits. Over the years I have come to the conclusion that there will be no meaningful movement toward social justice and real educational reform until there has been a significant transformation in the beliefs, attitudes, and actions of White Americans. As Malcolm X reminded us years ago, "We can't teach what we don't know, and we can't lead where we won't go."

The inner work of personal transformation has been the missing piece in the preparation of White teachers, and it is one of the central themes of this book. Too often we place White teachers in multicultural settings and expect them to behave in ways that are inconsistent with their own life experiences, socialization patterns, worldviews, and levels of racial identity development (Alba, 1990; Fine et al., 1997; Nieto, 1999, 2003; Sleeter, 1994; Vavrus, 2002). Too often we expect White teachers to be what they have not learned to be, namely, culturally competent professionals. I have attempted in this book to provide a conceptual framework whereby we can more adequately understand, support, and promote the personal transformation of White educators.

THE OUTER WORK OF SOCIAL TRANSFORMATION

As important as the inner work of personal growth is, however, it must be balanced with a vision of multicultural education as a process of social change and transformation (Banks, 2004; Sleeter, 2001). If we as White educators merely turn inward and deal only with our own needs for cultural awareness and racial identity development, we are in danger of perpetuating the kind of privileged non-engagement with the real issues of social justice that has characterized Whites for far too long (Sheets, 2000). The second major theme of the book, therefore, is an examination of the role White educators can and must play in understanding, decoding, and dismantling the dynamics of White dominance. Throughout the book I have attempted to hold in creative tension these two essential and inherently related themes: the personal transformation of White educators and the social transformation of the arrangements of White dominance. Each of these themes is a critical factor in any authentic movement toward the elimination of the achievement gap.

During one of my annual fund-seeking visits to Washington, DC, I discovered on a morning walk that the statue from the top of the Capitol dome had been removed by a large crane and placed in a congressional parking lot. One of the workers informed me that the statue, which is named "Freedom," was scheduled for major refurbishing before being returned to its perch above our nation's seat of power. I was pleased to discover that around the base of Freedom's form were inscribed the words *E Pluribus Unum.*

This scene presents a fitting image for a nation that is still attempting to live up to its founding principles. "Out of the Many, One" has remained an illusive vision for us as a people. Too often the political operatives wielding power beneath our nation's dome seem more intent on using our differences against us rather than inspiring us to embrace both our unity and our diversity. It seemed appropriate that we ought to regularly polish the face of Freedom and reread the words inscribed by generations past.

Our task as educators is similar to that of the craftspeople assigned to Freedom's face-lift. The conserving function of education is to inculcate into the minds and hearts of each new generation those fundamental values and principles that define our unique character as a nation. The transforming function of education, on the other hand, is to critically interpret those founding values in the light of ever-changing social realities and to continually challenge the discrepancies between our stated beliefs and our national behavior (Parker, 2003).

As multicultural educators we embody both the conserving and the transforming functions of education. In this sense our work is inherently political (Freire, 1970; Parker, 2003). We seek to continually renew and inform our students' commitment to the ideals of pluralistic democracy, and at the same time we diligently speak out when those ideals are violated in actual practice. Likewise, we teach our students the basic principles of "freedom and justice for all," and we seek to empower them to identify and address the many realities of injustice and inequality they see enacted in their everyday lives.

Among White educators I have observed considerable confusion and tentativeness in our willingness and ability to embrace these dual functions of education. In a scene that has been repeated many times in my workshops, a White middle school teacher came to me during a break in our session and said, "I feel really uncomfortable being here as a White person. When we talk about all of the racism and oppression that has happened to people of color in this nation, I feel guilty and blamed. I don't know what my role in discussions of race ought to be. As a White teacher I feel insecure, and I don't know if it's my place to bring these issues up with my students."

In this book I have attempted to avoid the "blame-and-shame" approach to multicultural education that has sometimes exacerbated the insecurities of White educators. It is important to acknowledge, however, that no matter how gentle and inclusive we may try to be, many White people will respond in ways similar to the teacher quoted above. In preparing White educators for both the personal and the social dimensions of transformation that must take place if we are to live and teach effectively within the context of racial diversity, it is essential that Whiteness "be re-negotiated as a productive force within the politics of difference" (Giroux, 1997b, p. 297). I have devoted considerable space throughout the text to exploring the relationship between Whiteness and social dominance, but I have attempted to do so in a way that unhooks us from the rhetoric of blame.

As White educators, we often suffer from the "dysconscious racism" that makes it difficult for us to see the full impact of our own social dominance (J. E. King, 1991). However, if we take seriously Cornel West's (1993b) challenge to "speak the truth to power," then we must face our feelings of inadequacy, discomfort, and guilt. We must seek to transform both ourselves and the social conditions of injustice that continue to stifle the potential of too many of our students from all racial, ethnic, cultural, and language groups. The goal for White educators is not to become "politically correct" in the simplistic and cynical tone that term has come to engender, but rather to become "personally conscious" in our role as concerned White educators committed to social healing and positive change.

And it is not only White educators who need to take on the inner and outer work of personal and social transformation; the challenge applies equally to our colleagues from other racial, ethnic, and cultural groups. As Nieto (1998) has pointed out from her extensive experience in multicultural teacher preparation:

> We cannot assume that, simply because of their marginal status in society, African American, Latino, Asian, and American Indian prospective and practicing teachers and others different from the majority can teach students from other backgrounds. . . . [Teachers] from backgrounds other than European American are also largely unprepared to teach students from groups other than their own. (p. 5.)

Many of the things I will say to and about White educators throughout this book could be equally applied to teachers from other racial and cultural groups. However, because Whites represent such a large majority of the teacher population, because we are often poorly prepared to engage the deep issues of multicultural teaching, because so many of us feel uncomfortable with our role as educators in diverse settings, and because we have an opportunity to make a unique and significant contribution to healing the wounds of past and present oppression, I have chosen here to specifically address my White colleagues.

ORGANIZATION OF BOOK

Throughout the book I have attempted to bridge the language of theory and the language of practice. The book is designed as a weaving fashioned from two textures of yarn: the texture of personal experiences and stories drawn from my many years in the field, and the texture of research drawn from the rich literature related to multicultural education and social justice (Banks & Banks, 2004). By intersecting the warp of practice with the woof of theory, I have attempted to achieve a level of relevance, interest, and meaningfulness for practicing and prospective teachers, while at the same time highlighting salient features of the academic literature related to issues of social dominance, racial identity development, and transformational teaching. The many anecdotes included in the text present the raw truth of lived experience and the validity of our many personal stories. Likewise, the numerous references to the research literature provide the collective conclusions that grow from more detached analysis. By thus weaving together the diverse textures of theory and practice, I have attempted to hold in creative tension both the personal and the social dimensions of transformation. Neither texture of yarn is more valuable than the other because each is essential to the overall strength and cohesion of our work as transformational leaders and educators.

In Chapter 1, I offer my own story of personal transformation. I describe how I grew from a state of almost complete ignorance and isolation concerning the realities of race and toward greater understanding of racism, social dominance, and the need for deep changes in our society. Chapter 2 provides a review of the literature related to social dominance and other theoretical constructs that can help us understand the methodologies of White supremacy. Chapter 3 offers a deeper examination of the roots of racism and social dominance, wherein three central components of the dominance paradigm are identified and deconstructed for the benefit of White educators who wish to critically examine their own personal and pedagogical assumptions regarding race and cultural differences.

Chapter 4 shifts the focus to a consideration of social action and change, exploring how White educators can effectively contribute to the process of healing and social transformation related to issues of race, dominance, and the role of White teachers in multicultural schools. Chapter 5 provides an overview of research related to racial identity development, detailing many of the central issues of personal transformation that face White teachers who wish to grow toward greater multicultural competence. Chapter 6 further explicates the process of personal transformation by setting forth a practitioner's model for mapping and supporting the formation of authentic and transformationist White racial identity.

Chapter 7, which is newly added to this second edition, carries the major themes of the book into the context of the classroom and current issues of school reform, highlighting the actual beliefs and practices of transformationist White teachers. The concluding chapter brings the personal and social dimensions of change together into a single transformative vision that can hopefully guide our work into the future. The central unifying intent throughout the book is to encourage, inspire, and inform White educators in our efforts to become a healing force in the lives of our students and a catalyst for change in the communities we serve.

FURTHER CONSIDERATIONS

Even though I have chosen to deal primarily with issues of race in this book, it must be acknowledged that similar processes of social dominance and oppression function across all major dimensions of human difference, including gender, religion, language, age, sexual orientation, social class, and ability. Partly from the need to achieve a manageable scope for the book, but primarily from the reality of race as a central marker in my own life, I have selected race as my focus here. Still, much of the analysis and many of the conclusions presented could be equally applied to other dimensions of diversity and social justice.

It must also be acknowledged that I cannot "prove" everything I say in this book. Much of what I share here comes from my experiences with the thousands of educators and students I encounter each year in my work throughout the United States and Australia. Their stories and their voices have informed and shaped my thinking and guided my reflections throughout the text, and occasionally they have led me beyond the horizons of established research in the field. At particular locations within the text I have chosen to enter this unmapped territory precisely because it offers rich possibilities for exploration and future research. What we have learned and documented to date has not led us to our desired goal of equity and social justice, so it is essential that we push beyond the edges of the known, to discover those places where healing and hope are still possible.

I have been inspired in my writing by the many passionately committed teachers I have met throughout the world and by the hundreds of letters and personal stories I have received from readers of the first edition of this book. I have seen the results of your extraordinarily good work in the bright eyes and ready smiles of students from all racial, ethnic, cultural, and language groups. There is much compassion, joy, deep learning, and transformation happening daily in classrooms throughout the world. By exploring in this book the painful processes and outcomes of racism and social dominance, I have intended not to overshadow this good work but hopefully to bring more of its healing light into the lives of children everywhere. In this spirit, I look forward to the day when we can stand together as educators and offer the actual outcomes of our teaching as indisputable evidence that we do, indeed, value *all* of our children. That day is not yet here.

CHAPTER 1

White Man Dancing: A Story of Personal Transformation

> It is time for a redefinition of White America. As our percentage of the population declines, our commitment to the future must change. . . . The future calls each of us to become partners in the dance of diversity, a dance in which everyone shares the lead. And because we have been separated by race and ethnicity for so long, we may feel awkward at first with the new moves. . . . But with a little help from our friends in other cultures, even White folks can learn to dance again, as we once did among the great stone circles of ancient Europe.
> —Gary R. Howard, "Whites in Multicultural Education"

Since I first penned these words in 1993 for a special multicultural issue of the *Phi Delta Kappan*, edited by James A. Banks, many people have asked me about the dance of White America. Thirty years ago, when I started the REACH Center for Multicultural Education, some people challenged whether a White person ought to be involved in this work. Now that the movement has matured, and REACH has a diverse corps of trainers who work with schools internationally, the inclusion of Whites is more accepted and usually actively encouraged. The question remains, though: Why would any White person choose to become involved?

As I travel throughout the United States and Australia, people continue to ask how I became committed to multicultural education. What experiences brought me to this place? What lessons can other White Americans learn? In the reflections that follow, I have tried to deal with these questions in a personal way, piecing together the strains of my own life's song, looking for the lessons that have drawn me into the dance.

THE LUXURY OF IGNORANCE

I was born White and have been that way for more than 60 years. The first 18 of those years can best be described as a period of "cultural encapsulation" (J. A. Banks, 1994). Since I had never met a person who wasn't White, had never experienced the "other," race for me was a nonrelevant concept. In my youth, I had no conscious awareness of anything that might be called "racial identity." Like water to a fish, or the air we breathe (Tatum, 2003), Whiteness to me was the centerpiece of a constant and undifferentiated milieu, unnoticed in its normalcy.

It wasn't until my senior year in high school that I discovered my Whiteness. A White male friend, who was going out with an African American student from another school, asked if I wanted to join them on a double date with one of her friends, also Black. This was the first time I had ever been invited to dip my toes in the river of racial consciousness. It was the first intrusion into my white-washed world. I was afraid. I was confused. I was curious.

As for most of my fellow White Americans growing up in suburbia in the 1950s, people of color had existed only on the distant periphery of my social reality. "Amos and Andy," Tonto in "The Lone Ranger," and clips of civil rights activities on the evening news were my only tenuous connections with the other America. And even these limited images were, of course, coming through several layers of White media filtering, with all the inevitable prejudice and racism intact.

This simple invitation to meet a new person, to go on a date with an African American woman, shook loose one of the basic linchpins of my social isolation. It is interesting that my initial response was fear. Fear is the classic White American reaction to any intrusion into our cultural capsule. What will happen to me? Will I be safe? What will other White people think of me? What will "the other" think of me? How do I act? What do I say? Will I survive? I was overwhelmed by an emotional flood of narcissistic and xenophobic trivia.

I did go on the date, and I had a good time. This young woman enabled me to make a human connection across the barrier of race that had been constructed around both of our lives. With neither our awareness nor our consent, we had both been born into a society which had already decided that our lives should not touch. Together, in the simple act of coming together to share a good time, we broke through that wall, creating one small crack in the artificial barrier of racial isolation.

Reflecting back on this experience, I realize that members of the dominant group in any society do not necessarily have to know anything about those people who are not like them. For our survival and the carrying on of the day-to-day activities of our lives, most White Americans do not have to engage in any meaningful personal connection with people who are different. This privileged isolation is not a luxury available to people who live outside of dominance and must, for their survival, understand the essential social nuances of those in power. The luxury of ignorance reinforces and perpetuates White isolation (see Chapter 3).

This one connection I made in high school with a person outside my own race symbolizes an essential step for any dominant culture person who wishes to grow beyond the limits of encapsulation. We must become aware of both our differentness from, and our relatedness to, other people and their cultural realities. Whether we deepen in our awareness and continue to grow through such experiences, or merely shrink back into the safety of isolation, is determined by our reaction to the inevitable fear of stepping outside the boundary of ignorance.

BAPTISM BY FIRE

My second major lesson about Whiteness came with moving from Seattle to attend Yale in 1964. This lesson happened not because Yale was particularly diverse at that time but because New Haven itself was such a hotbed of racial conflict and civil rights activity. I came to Yale with the Bible in one hand and a copy of conservative Republican presidential candidate Barry Goldwater's platform in the other, foreshadowing by four decades what we now see in the Christian right's fusion of reactionary politics and mind-numbing religiosity. Needless to say, I was not at that time a likely candidate for any radical shift in racial consciousness.

However, it was these same adolescent spiritual stirrings, coupled with the starched and ironed Presbyterian doctrine of salvation through works, that led me in my freshman year to begin working with young inner-city Black and Hispanic kids through a YMCA program. One afternoon a week, I would walk six blocks and several light years of social reality away from Yale to spend a few hours with my group of preteen males. My job was to be a big brother for them, create fun activities, go to the gym together, and help keep the guys off the streets and out of trouble. Their job, as it turned out, was to teach me more and deeper lessons than I learned in four years at Yale.

These young men lived in "the Hill," one of New Haven's most impoverished neighborhoods and an area that had been targeted for the mixed blessings of urban renewal. From the perspective of most Yalies, the Hill was a place you didn't go, a dangerous world, festering with crime and social disintegration. For the social scientists and Great Society bureaucrats, it was a treasure trove for research and grant opportunities. All the demographics of race and poverty pointed in the right direction to make a strong case for "cultural deprivation," that most unfortunate and inaccurate of terms that was so popular in the 1960s version of liberal paternalism.

For me, the Hill was where Tyrone, Ruben, Charlie, Bruce, and the other guys in the group lived. I was naive and idealistic, full of missionary zeal, wanting to help in some way. I didn't understand the larger social realities that had created this neighborhood as a "ghetto." I was invited into the homes of my group members, met their extended families, and came to see the Hill as a place where concerned and worried parents, often working against great odds, were trying to give their kids a decent chance for a good life.

It was only gradually that I came to understand the larger American reality that the Hill represented. I met other Yalies who had dedicated their undergraduate years to civil rights organizing in the South and in New Haven. I met Black and Hispanic community leaders who extended and deepened the reeducation I was receiving from my young group members. I began to steer my academic program toward courses that would give me the intellectual tools to understand racism, poverty, and the historical, political, and economic manipulations that had led to the creation of the Hill neighborhoods of our nation.

In the middle of my Yale career I got married, and Lotus and I moved into an apartment on Howard Avenue, in the heart of the Hill. The lessons deepened as we lived there and as the urban struggle of the 1960s intensified. During three consecutive "long hot summers," our neighborhood was racked with riots and burning. National Guard troops, with their heavy weapons and armored vehicles, became a regular sight on the streets of the Hill, as was true in hundreds of other neighborhoods across the country. Lotus and I worked together with our neighbors in programs for kids, trying to give them some sense of a normal summer, safe from the violence, the burning, and the military occupation of their streets.

The last fires of my New Haven days came in the spring of 1968, just after the assassination of Dr. Martin Luther King, Jr., when several blocks around our apartment burned to the ground. I remember my former Yale roommates calling from campus that night to ask how we were doing. They had heard about the riots on the news and were worried about us. "We're fine," I said. "Just watching the burning out on our back fire escape, and it looks like our apartment will be OK."

Some 40 years later, these memories of fire and frightened children and the vast social and psychological distance between Yale and the Hill remain as some of the most powerful images of my life. How would I be different today if I had never ventured into the Hill? Who would I have become had I not been baptized in the fires of that particular time? My reality was fundamentally and unalterably changed during those years. My politics shifted from far right to far left. My religious beliefs were challenged and transformed. The single-truth simplicities of my Christian fundamentalism were melted down in the heat of that reality. I lost the faith of my childhood but found a vision to guide the rest of my life. I could no longer be the self-righteous missionary with the answers for others. I could only hope to be one small part of a seemingly overwhelming struggle for healing and social justice.

How can White Americans, those who have never been touched viscerally by the realities of race, break out of their cultural isolation and ignorance? It was fire that burned away the walls of my encapsulation. It was engagement with real people in a context totally different from my former life in the suburbs. Something powerful has to happen to us and for us, something we cannot dismiss. Yet even the deep changes of this intense time were only the beginning of my personal transformation.

BRINGING IT ALL BACK HOME

I didn't realize it at the time, but this naive missionary period was merely the tentative beginning of a long journey toward cultural competence and multicultural awareness. The missionary phase began to dissipate as I gradually realized I was receiving more than I was giving. I was amazed that I was welcomed and treated so well by my neighbors in the Hill, considering their painful history with most of the White world. I was invited into the life of the community and given incredible opportunities to grow beyond the limits of my White ignorance. I don't know how conscious my Black and Hispanic colleagues were in their efforts, but it was as if they had decided together, "Here's a White guy we can perhaps educate. Let's allow him in and see how much he can take. Then we can help him move on to the real work he has to do."

One of the culminating experiences of my New Haven period was to work as the only White staff person in a Black Identity and Leadership Summer Camp for inner-city high school students. A close friend, who was a social worker and a leader in the Black community, asked me to take on the assignment of "being a White person for the kids to react to as they work out the issues of their Black identity." I thought this would perhaps be the most intense experience I could possibly add to the riots and other stresses of life in the Hill, so, in the true spirit of the 1960s, I took the job.

It was here that I was introduced to the issues of White privilege and complicity, which were not academic concepts to be argued about in the antiseptic pages of professional journals but a matter of daily pain and awareness for the students and the staff in that summer program. They put the truth in my face and they taught me well. In a sense, I was placed in the role of representing all of White America for that summer, and it was not a comfortable job. They taught me about the 500-year history that exponentially increased the likelihood that I would be a student at Yale and they would not. They confronted me with the fact that even though my family was hanging by a toenail to the lower rungs of the middle class, our limited success had been achieved through the land we stole from the American Indians and the labor we stole from Blacks, Asians, and Hispanics. This is part of the standard multicultural mantra today, but 40 years ago it was a new and powerful awareness for me. Indeed, my mother's family farm in Minnesota, which has been one of the cornerstones of my personal history and connection to culture, is built on land stolen from the Ojibway people only 30 years before my great-grandparents acquired it.

The students also reminded me that "you may live in the Hill now, and hang out with Black people, but you're at Yale and you can go back there whenever you want. We were born in the Hill and don't have any other place to go. It's not an option for us *not* to be Black, that's what we are 24 hours a day for our whole lives. If you wanted to, if things got too heavy for you here, or when you graduate, you can walk away from this thing and never look back. We can't do that." None of my Yale professors taught me these realities of White privilege, yet young Black students in the late 1960s were quite articulate on the subject. They were my allies and my most influential teachers. White Americans desperately need this kind of reeducation, and it is indeed a blessing when someone takes the time to provide it, as these young Black leaders did for me.

My missionary mentality was further eroded and essentially obliterated by the arrival in New Haven of Black Power politics and the growing presence of the Black Panthers. It was exciting to be in the middle of these historic developments. The passion for change was palpable on the streets. The struggle was real and many people were willing to risk everything for it. In the midst of the pain and the fear, there was profound hope, and both the Panthers and the ideology of Black Power embodied this rejuvenation of energy and spirit. The line was drawn and there was no going back.

Involvement in these events of the late 1960s stimulated an important step in the evolution of my White identity development. Before my immersion in the urban revolution at that time, I had no way of perceiving the power and willingness of White America to maintain its own dominance. I did not know the extent to which Whites in power would subvert their own expressed values of justice and liberty in order to destroy those outside their group who justly claimed access to those same values. This was not the America I had read about in my high school textbooks, that idealized and just nation that too many White folks still trust to be real. It was only through living with people outside my particular fishbowl that I was able to finally perceive the true nature of my previously invisible milieu. Through their eyes I came to see the water of White dominance as a highly selective poison that continually steals the lifeblood from those people who have not been marked with the genetic code of Whiteness.

ADVENTURES OF AN ANTI-RACIST RACIST

These experiences in New Haven led me to a profound shift in consciousness that has guided my career for the past four decades. Helped along by some strong feedback from Black Power leaders and friends in the Black Panthers, I came to see that my real work was not in the Hill neighborhood but back home with my own folks. The core of the problem was in White America, and if I wanted to help excise the cancer of racism, I had to go to the source of the tumor. In the spring of 1969, my Black colleagues and neighbors challenged me to take what I had learned from them and find a way to teach those lessons within the context of the White community. Together we buried the missionary and gave birth to the subversive.

I was not enthusiastic about this new assignment. For me, the action was in the inner city. That was where I had come of age and where the most profound experiences of my young adulthood had taken place. The Black community had been the laboratory where young people and community leaders had performed the alchemy of my personal transformation. The Hill had been the altar of fiery baptism that forever changed the way I saw the world. I didn't want to go back home and deal with my racist Uncle John, the Brady Bunch, and the rest of Ozzie-and-Harriet America.

I had entered the period of rejecting my racial identity. I had learned what it meant to be White in America, and I didn't want to have anything to do with it. I had broken the seal on my own cultural encapsulation, blown away many of the old images, and didn't want to be identified with White folks anymore. I had opened the door on understanding my own complicity, privilege, and racism and wanted to put this in the face of other White folks who had not yet paid their dues. I wanted to be different, not one of them.

I did accept the challenge, however, and went back home to work within the White community. Needless to say, my early attempts at sharing these new insights were not often warmly received by the unknowing

White people who were the unfortunate recipients of my wrath. It was clear to them I had a chip on my shoulder. Working in my first career, which was as an assistant minister in a large White church, my basic pedagogical approach to parishioners was, "What you need to know is that you're a racist." This was the typical strategy for most "White Racism Awareness Training" workshops in the early 1970s, and I was among the more energetic practitioners of that particular style.

It is no mystery that my career in the church was short-lived. The passions that fueled my ministry ran upstream against the safe liberal theology and politics of the senior ministers and most of the congregation. In the community of White affluence to which I had been called, I was allowed three short years to spread my particularly caustic version of the social gospel. I concluded at the time that many White Americans were quite content with "Father Knows Best" and the other programmed myths of their cultural encapsulation. They did not want to switch channels to see the world through my eyes. The realities of the Hill were once again light years away, and I felt wounded and alone in my first attempts to penetrate the dominant reality of my own people.

By the time I entered my second career, that of education, I had begun to mature in my understanding of both the message and the messenger. My work in the church could be characterized as a period of rejecting my own Whiteness and confronting other White people with theirs. The next period, which has continued in some aspects even to the present, can best be described as a time of working on "the reeducation of White America." I came to see that the awareness and growth I had gained in the concentrated, high-voltage context of New Haven from 1964 to 1969 could not be transmitted directly to other White folks who had not lived similar realities. They needed to be engaged in an educational process that would help mediate the transition to a different perspective, a different way of being White (see Chapters 5 and 6).

Still, in keeping with my 1960s commitment to mind-altering intensity, I began my education career by teaching American history to 13-and 14-year-olds in a White rural community. In a seemingly idyllic setting nestled among the foothills of the Cascade Mountains of Western Washington, Black families had been burned out of their homes when they tried to move into the area. There were murmurings of the Klan's presence a few miles down the road. My students were much like I had been at their age—totally oblivious to the larger multicultural story of their country. In them I saw reflected the same cultural isolation that had dominated my youth. Teaching in that middle school was a full turning of the circle of my life, a homecoming of sorts, and I wanted desperately to find a way to reach my students with the lessons I had learned.

This was a pivotal time for me, and perhaps instructive for a larger view of White multicultural identity development. Following the church experience, I had moved to this rural setting in the hills and invested five years of my life turning inward, living simply with my wife on the land, having children, building a home, earning a subsistence living through physical labor that had nothing to do with either my academic preparation or my commitment to ending racism. It was a time of incubation, softening, and consolidation of all that I had experienced in the firestorm of the New Haven years and the frigid climate of the church. I needed this time to heal from the harshness of what I had seen, yet even in this withdrawal from activism I was exercising a form of White privilege.

After five years on the land, I emerged ready to be engaged again. Having gained some measure of rest and renewal, I could not avoid the inner voice that called me to be involved in change. I went back to school and wrote a thesis on multicultural education in monocultural schools, which made a case for teaching about diversity even in schools where racial diversity was not evident. Next, I procured funding to develop classroom strategies and materials aimed at multiculturalizing the teaching of American history for predominantly White populations. Following this came the design of a teacher-training program to help White educators reconceptualize their curriculum and their pedagogy from a multicultural perspective. All of this developmental activity formed the prototype for what was later to become the REACH Center approach to multicultural education, which has now been implemented in all 50 states, as well as Australia.

In relation to White multicultural identity development, I had now moved into a time of positive activity. I was searching for a method and a focus for sharing the experiences and learnings gained during my immersion in New Haven. The bitterness about my Whiteness and the harshness in my approach to other White people were beginning to dissipate. I wanted to invite other White folks into the worldview that had been given to me. Rather than beating my students and colleagues over the head with their Whiteness and their ignorance, I wanted to find ways to help them break out of their own encapsulation. This positive engagement with other White people in a process of mutual growth provided a healing balance to my earlier strategy of frontal assault. I was beginning to realize that the appropriate response to learning about the realities of White racism in America is not rejection, guilt, denial, or distancing from ourselves as White people, but rather direct action with others for positive change.

It is important to point out that none of the multicultural growth I had been able to achieve up to this point would have been possible without the support and honesty of many friends and colleagues of color. Our current diversity jargon makes much of the need for White folks to become allies for people of color in the battle for equity and social justice. This is an important issue and essential for systemic change, but I have discovered that the road of alliance must run both ways. Without my allies from other cultures, I would still be swimming in the suburban fishbowl of White ignorance. The young people in New Haven, my neighbors and friends there, the community leaders who challenged me, the highly diverse staff and trainers at the REACH Center in Seattle, my colleagues across the United States and around the world—all of these diverse people have contributed to my education and transformation as a White person. White identity development is intrinsically tied to direct engagement across the cultural and racial divide.

SHAPING AN AUTHENTIC WHITE IDENTITY

In recent years, as I have entered my sixties, the rhythms of my journey have been shifting and the music has been changing in subtle ways, calling for new steps in the dance of White identity. Several experiences have been catalysts for this new time. At a National Service Learning Conference in Minneapolis, where I participated in a panel discussion on diversity issues, a White high school student in our group told a story that has continued to echo in my heart. She described her involvement in a summer multicultural leadership camp, where each evening students from a different ethnic group were asked to share a creative presentation of their cultural and historical perspectives. First, there was African American night, followed by Hispanic night, then Asian American night, Native American night, and finally, on the last evening of the camp, it was White night. She talked about how emotionally draining it had been for her to observe each of the previous presentations, repeatedly being exposed to the painful experiences with racism, oppression, and genocide these other groups had endured, all at the hands of White people. When the time came for the White students to present their story, she could not participate. "I felt like ripping off my White skin," she said.

After hearing her story, I was not able to free myself from the image of this young woman's painful revulsion in the face of her ethnic identity. I thought about my own teaching and about the multicultural materials I had developed for teachers and students over the years. Even though my approach had softened from the "up against the wall" style of my church career, I saw that nothing I had done could adequately respond to this young woman's troubled emotions. In fact, as I realized later, I had probably placed untold numbers of White students and teachers in exactly the same position. Through the REACH Center, we had distributed thousands of copies of our *Ethnic Perspectives Series* of student books, including *An African American Perspective, An Asian American Perspective, An Hispanic/ Latino Perspective,* and *An American Indian Perspective.* Like those ethnic evenings at the summer camp, these books tell the story of racism and oppression perpetrated by the dominant culture, including much of the information that has not been included in commercial textbooks. I wondered how many of the White students in REACH classrooms all across the country had wanted to rip away their ethnic identity after being exposed to our books.

From this and similar stories from other White Americans, I have come to realize that our efforts to "reeducate White America" must go beyond the mere recitation of other groups' suffering at the hands of White people. It must also go beyond "appreciating other cultures." And it must go beyond acknowledging our own racism, complicity, and privilege. Confronting the realities of my collective history has been a necessary step in the evolution of my White multicultural identity, but it has not been sufficient. Embracing the negative aspects of Whiteness does not suffice as a cultural identity. Oppression has been a part of my history, but it does not fully define me. For myself, my children, and my White students and colleagues, I want to provide more than mere acknowledgment of our legacy of hate. I want to provide more than valuing and appreciating other peoples' culture—and more than working to overcome the realities of racism and oppression. These are necessary aspects of an emerging White identity, but they do not create a whole and authentic person.

The broader and beginning strokes of a larger picture have begun to come into focus for me only in the past few years. After a year-long sabbatical, during which I was immersed in different cultures around the world, I found myself alone one night on a moonlit beach at Byron Bay, on the east coast of Australia. I had just completed a whirlwind tour of Aboriginal Australia, the guest of a friend who is an elder and caretaker of the land in the spiritual tradition of her people on the north coast of New South Wales. She had taken me to many of the important places, the prominent physical features of the land that are central to the stories and songlines of her tradition. I had met one of her teachers, a woman in her nineties, who told me stories as old as the land itself. As I was drawn into their world, the stories came to life in the spirit of the landscape. Myth and magic merged with my own reality, and the borders grew fuzzy. Each night I awoke with vivid dreams dancing in the quietest predawn hours, the time when my friend had told me the spirit messengers were most active. I seemed to be getting more than the standard tourist excursion.

It was after three weeks of this intensity that I stood alone under the full moon on the beach at Byron Bay. I had said goodbye to my friend and was flying out the next morning. As I watched the playful mutual caress of moonlight and seafoam in the surf, I thought of home 8,000 miles across the Pacific. I wondered how I might translate my Aboriginal immersion experience over that immense distance. More importantly, I pondered how I might apply it to the home within myself. The lesson that came to me then, and has been deepening since, is the realization that for many years, ever since my New Haven days, I had been relying on other people's cultures to provide me with a sense of meaning. Life had been most real and vital for me when I was engaged in intense multicultural experiences. I felt most alive when I was immersed in a cultural reality different from my own. Much of my sense of identity had been forged in diverse cultural contexts separate from White America.

I did not see this as negative, merely incomplete. My experience was not what we normally think of as the "wannabe" phenomenon, which is a typical pitfall for many White folks who have a longing for culture. My motivation had not been to *become* an Aboriginal person, or a Black American, or a Native American. My particular issue, as it came to me at Byron Bay, was that I had centered much of my sense of self on my experiences with people outside my own cultural group. This had worked well for the formation of multicultural awareness, but it left a large void in terms of understanding my own culture as a White person. I saw that my intense identification with the "other" had been part of a continuing effort to distance myself from the distasteful aspects of being White. I had spent my adult life looking for meaning in other people's cultures, and now it was time to find it in my own.

Not so coincidentally, the last stop on my sabbatical world journey was the British Isles, ancestral homeland for my father's side of the family. Here my wife, Lotus, and I joined a small band of fellow travelers in a pilgrimage to many of the ancient sacred sites of the old Celts, including Glastonbury, Stonehenge, and Iona. Led by a wonderful young man, who is a storyteller, dancer, and contemporary Scottish bard, we danced and sang and storied our way across the countryside. Through his passion, and the power of the places we visited, I was able to get a feel for the magic of the Isles in the time before the Romans and the Church came to do what the British and the rest of Europe later did to Indigenous people around the world. The Celtic tradition, like that of Native Americans and countless other groups, was nearly decimated by the invaders, and Christian churches were superimposed on many of the old places of Celtic worship and wonder. In spite of these acts of desecration, however, I found that many of the stone circles remain today as living testimonials to the earthy vibrance and mystical vision of my cultural ancestors.

Upon arriving at Stonehenge, we found the central attraction had been fenced off, inaccessible to the tourists who had proved too disrespectful in past visits. Fortunately for us, our bard-in-residence had some ancestral pull with the guards, and we were able to enter after closing time to spend the entire night with the giant stones themselves. We played our instruments and performed our folk dances for this august audience of silent, watchful witnesses. The wind was strong that night, and blackened clouds ran across the Salisbury hills, mirroring above the flow of our dancing below.

This was a magic night for me. I felt the presence of the ancient Celts who had chanted here their prayers to earth and sky, performing their rituals through the sacred geometry of these same stones. The circle was drawn, and we were inside the space created for us, the place designed to teach us about ourselves, our relationship to each other, and our connection to everything else outside the ring of stone. This is the function of culture—to provide a context, a circle of meaning, and a sense of relationship to all of life.

This night in Stonehenge seemed to answer the question posed for me earlier, half a world away at Byron Bay: "How do I incorporate into my own identity these intense experiences with other cultures?" I discovered that I do so by finding a deep connection with personal culture that is indigenous to my own heritage. At Stonehenge, I embraced my Whiteness, all aspects of it. I found my rhythm, danced through the night, and felt at home.

Only recently have I thought more about the fence. I was shocked when I first saw it and thought we could not get in to be among the stones. Our history as White people has been like that. Barriers of dominance and racism and the pressures of assimilation have neutralized our connection to culture. We have collectively destroyed other cultures, buried our own, and denied the histories of both. My whole life, since I was 18, had been an effort to rebuild the bridges to other people's cultures. At Stonehenge, I penetrated the fence that had separated me from my own.

Subsequent to my sabbatical tour, we have now written *A European American Perspective* book to compliment our REACH *Ethnic Perspectives Series*. This student text acknowledges the history of White dominance but goes beyond that to highlight the many White men and women who have fought, in all times and places, to limit and resist the legacy of racism. The book validates the fact that White people have culture, and it explores the highly diverse ethnic roots of White Americans. In addition, we now include a White American presentation in our training events, to reinforce the understanding that we are all part of the social justice agenda. We find that these efforts have rekindled a fire in the minds and hearts of White participants and students, who feel included at last in the circle of culture and change, not isolated in the dancehall of dominance and blame.

THE DANCE CONTINUES

Learning the dance of diversity is not easy for White Americans. There are complex moves and many ways to lose the step. Before my lessons could begin, I first had to break out of cultural encapsulation and isolation, which entailed much initial shock in the New Haven years, followed by continuing waves of seismic dislocation of my former reality. I began to see myself as Blacks, Hispanics, and others outside my group saw me, both collectively and personally. I had to face the history of White dominance. I had to confront my own ignorance, and I often tripped over my own and others' feet as I felt my way into the choreography of the larger dance.

In order to continue the lessons and learn the more difficult steps, I had to acknowledge my own complicity and privilege, as well as the racism in myself and my family. I had to learn to move with some degree of grace and style to these new rhythms, without stumbling over guilt, denial, or the rejection of my own Whiteness. Then, as the tempo heated up and I began to feel the groove, I wanted to get other White folks into the dance. To do this, I had to learn to be an instructor myself, finding a way to share what I had learned and to help heal the pain of the past.

Today, as the dance of diversity continues for me, I want to take more time to think about the music. Where is it coming from? Am I dancing to my own rhythm, or merely moving to someone else's tune echoing in my heart? I find myself listening more now for my own inner music. In my work with other people, I am slowing down the pace and inviting them to go deeper into their understanding of themselves and their relationship to realities outside their own. I am less patient with our diversity jargon and the surface strains of the old multicultural tunes, which sometimes push us to impose our own assumptions rather than waiting for the larger truths to emerge. I want to explore the more subtle tones of the music now, the nuances and complexities created by our vast differences and similarities as human beings. The lines we have drawn around race and culture seem too simplistic to speak to the incredible diversity of our actual lives.

I know the dance of White identity will continue to change and deepen for me. The choreography is a work in progress. Each new step I learn brings me closer to my unique place on the dance floor, helps me find my personal harmony, and guides the creation of a new way of being White, one that is both authentically connected to my own history and finely tuned to the rich mixture of sound and beat that is multicultural America. It is this new dance that has inspired me to share the reflections included in this book and to search for new avenues to healing that will transcend the limitations of our past rhetoric and best intentions.

CHAPTER 2

White Dominance and the Weight of the West

Deference to the physical superlative, a preference for the scent of our own clan: a thousand anachronisms dance down the strands of our DNA from a hidebound tribal past, guiding us toward the glories of survival, and some vainglories as well. If we resent being bound by these ropes, the best hope is to seize them out like snakes by the throat, look them in the eye, and own up to the venom.

—Barbara Kingsolver, *High Tide in Tucson*

During a multicultural workshop in Austin, Texas, a White elementary teacher, with a tone of intense frustration in her voice, said to the group, "I don't understand all of this talk about differences. Each of my little kindergarten students comes to me with the same stuff. It doesn't matter whether they're Black, Hispanic, or White, they each have a brain, a body, and a family. They each get the same curriculum. I treat them all alike. And yet, by the end of the year, and as I watch them move up through the grades, the Blacks and Hispanics fall behind and the White kids do better. They all start with the same basic equipment. What happens?"

I wondered how best to respond to the complexities underlying this teacher's naïve assumptions. There is so much that needs to be said about the notion that all children come to us with "the same stuff." I wanted to engage her in a discussion of the personal and cultural histories that each of her students brings to the classroom. These histories are not the same, yet they profoundly influence the educational process. I wanted to discuss the institutional practices that systematically favor certain racial, economic, and language groups, while negatively influencing others. I wanted to explore with her the 500-year history of racism and cultural genocide in the United States, which has had a devastating impact on the lives of many of her students and their families. I wanted to share with her the many lessons of race privilege and oppression I had learned from my Black and Hispanic neighbors in New Haven during the 1960s (see Chapter 1). In short, I wanted to abandon the "Introduction to Multicultural Curriculum" presentation I had been asked to deliver and shift to a deeper and more fundamental theme related to the history of social dominance in the United States.

REFLECTIONS IN THE EYE OF A SNAKE

As a White educator, I find it difficult to approach the topic of White dominance. I know that many of my White colleagues are tired of hearing about it. The litany of past sins committed by Whites against people of other races and cultures echoes in our ears, and we resist yet another recitation of this old and damning chant. We are tempted to cry out, "Enough! I know this story and I don't need to hear it again." Even those of us who are actively engaged in the work of social justice, and committed to more equitable educational outcomes for all of our students, still tire of being seen as the demons of history and the omnipresent oppressors of those who are not White.

Yet I also know that the naiveté evidenced by the teacher in Texas represents too many of my White colleagues. In my 30 years of working with educators in the United States and Australia, I have often heard sentiments similar to those expressed by this teacher. I continue to ask: How is it possible, with so much research and information available about multicultural issues today, that prospective educators can complete their entire teacher education and certification program without gaining a deeper grasp of social reality? Even though we sometimes may be tempted to close the discussion about White dominance, we have a responsibility to our students to assure that we and our colleagues remain open to ever deeper levels of awareness. It is the unexamined nature of White dominance that is often our problem (Fine et al., 1997). If our examination and understanding of the root causes of social inequality are too shallow, then our approach to corrective action will necessarily be superficial and ineffective (Sleeter, 1996). If we do not face dominance, we may be predisposed to perpetuate it.

Students, parents, and colleagues of color have repeatedly called for greater racial and cultural awareness on the part of White educators. Their voices challenge us to catch up with our own history by acknowledging the reality of past and present racism and dominance. As I seek to address this challenge in the present chapter, a single question looms large: How do I be anti-racist without appearing anti-White? I have found in my work that most White educators want to overcome the effects of dominance. We want to end racism rather than perpetuate it. Yet I have also found that many White educators, like the naive teacher in Texas, have not engaged in a sufficiently deep analysis of the root causes and dynamics of dominance.

Using Kingsolver's imagery from the opening quote to this chapter, many of my colleagues have never looked directly into the eyes of the snake of White dominance, and when invited to do so, they feel blamed rather than enlightened. And even those of us who have tried to stare down that viper are often uncomfortable with the reflection of ourselves we discover there, and we shy away from further confrontations or deeper learning. As Levine (1996) points out, "The quest to understand the past and the present in their full complexity and ambiguity can be discomfiting and even threatening" (p. xvii).

It is important to remember as we embark on this complex and sometimes uncomfortable journey into greater understanding that the "enemy" is dominance itself, not White people. This distinction becomes blurred at times precisely because of the overwhelming convergence of Whiteness and dominance in Western nations. Education in the West is the focus of this book, and in this context the overarching presence of dominance has been related to the establishment of European hegemony. If we were to broaden the focal point and look at the universal history of human suffering caused by arrangements of dominance and racism, there are many stories to be told, and the villains have not always been White. My intent here is to encourage meaningful discourse about Whiteness and social dominance in Western educational settings without becoming lost in the cycles of blame, guilt, anger, and denial that have so often in the past prevented honest engagement of these issues (Chavez-Chavez & O'Donnell, 1998).

SOCIAL DOMINANCE IN RESEARCH AND THEORY

A broad range of educational and social science research converges on the issue of social dominance. The study of dominance is related to research on issues such as prejudice, stereotyping, discrimination, racism, sexism, neoclassical elitism theory, social identity theories, and work in the field of political socialization (Sidanius & Pratto, 1993). Although a full review of the literature related to social dominance is beyond the scope of this book (Sniderman, Tetlock, & Carmines, 1993), my interest here is to introduce those concepts and findings that relate most directly to preparing White educators for the work of understanding and unraveling dominance in educational settings.

Minimal Group Paradigm

Research by Tajfel (1970) suggests that even superficial and seemingly meaningless distinctions between individuals can become the basis for prejudicial attitudes and discriminatory behaviors. Using Tajfel's minimal group paradigm, L. Howard and Rothbart (1980) conducted studies with college students wherein artificial and arbitrary distinctions were manufactured by the experimenters, informing each subject of his or her identity as either an "overestimator" or "underestimator" of the number of dots projected briefly on a screen. Observing their colleagues in a series of tasks, subjects were asked to allocate rewards to pairs of individuals, who were also labeled by their group status. When the pairs included one in-group member and one out-group member, the subjects systematically favored their own group.

The minimal group paradigm suggests that human beings tend to demonstrate discriminatory in-group and out-group dynamics even when there is an extremely limited basis for drawing distinctions between members of the groups. As teachers, we often witness this process in our classrooms. In a recent workshop with students from two neighboring high schools in the same rural, predominantly White town in upstate New York, the lesson of minimal group distinctions was brought home to me in a rather humorous way. Even though the two schools were virtually indistinguishable demographically, the students from one seemed to invest a great deal of energy in perpetuating a stereotype of students from the other school as a "bunch of hicks." During the workshop this issue of "degrees of hickness" was vigorously debated by students from both schools, with the tension and volume in the room rising as each new attack or counterattack further denigrated the members of the opposing group. Determined not to lose the workshop to the heat of such a seemingly insignificant battle, my co-facilitator and I finally called a break and discussed how we might use the "hick" issue as an entree into our intended discussion of race and gender stereotypes. The perfect teachable moment came when one of the few African American students in the workshop, a young woman who had recently moved to this small town from an urban and highly multicultural neighborhood, said to me, "Mr. Howard, I don't see what all this hassle is about. As far as I'm concerned, they're *all* a bunch of hicks."

This story illustrates two basic lessons of minimal group theory: (1) People tend to draw distinctions between themselves as individuals and groups, even if the distinctions are essentially meaningless in a larger context, and (2) having drawn these distinctions, we then ascribe values of superiority and inferiority to the various in-groups and out-groups we ourselves have created. When we add to this process the existence of a powerful "visible marker" such as race, we are left with patterns of intergroup relations that are extremely resistant to change (Rothbart & John, 1993).

The implications of minimal group theory are burdensome for those of us concerned with achieving more equitable interactions and outcomes in the classroom. If human beings are by nature predisposed to categorize and negatively discriminate against perceived out-groups, even when the basis for that differentiation is trivial and meaningless, then it might appear overwhelmingly difficult to reduce group-based biases related to more significant issues of human difference such as race, gender, social class, religion, ability, and sexual orientation. The minimal group paradigm raises a cautionary flag for us as educators, signaling both the difficulty and the necessity of working toward greater intergroup harmony (C.A.M. Banks, 2005).

Social Positionality

Researchers in the area of social positionality have provided additional clarification regarding the issue of dominance (Rosaldo, 1989). They have demonstrated that human beings tend to draw distinctions not only in terms of in-group and out-group but also in terms of dominance and subordination. How we view the world, how we construct reality, how we ascribe meaning and value to our lives are intimately connected to our position within social and historical hierarchies of dominance and subordination (Rosaldo, 1989). Social positionality has both subjective and objective dimensions. The subjective dimension relates to how I see myself and how others see me. The objective dimension relates to my social position in terms of more quantitative and observable measures, such as income, education level, or job title. The issue of positionality helps clarify the discussion of White collective identity. From the perspective of those members of society who are *not* White, it is quite clear, both subjectively and objectively, that Whites have been collectively allocated disproportionate amounts of power, authority, wealth, control, and dominance. However, for me as an individual White person, subjectively experiencing my own reality, I may or may not feel dominant. I may or may not perceive myself as belonging to a collective group defined by Whiteness.

It is from the conceptual frame of social positionality and collective identity that we can better understand and deconstruct typical comments from White participants in multicultural workshops, such as "I never owned slaves" or "I didn't kill Indians." As White people experiencing the world from our social position of dominance, we often fail, on an individual level, to identify with the collective group history that has been the foundation for establishing our dominance. In a recent corporate diversity workshop, for example, a White male bank president from Iowa was having trouble understanding the relationship between White collective identity and dominance. After listening to the collective images of Whiteness shared by Black, Hispanic, and Asian participants in the workshop, he gradually began to grasp the powerful impact of his own social positionality. His comment to the group was, "I feel like I'm a fish who just discovered water. I've been swimming so long in dominance that I wasn't aware of it." His personal revelation is echoed by Sleeter's (1996) assessment of her social positionality as a White woman: "The racism I was raised with was grounded in taken-for-granted acceptance of White people as the center of the universe" (p. 19).

Social positionality for Whites in Western societies has afforded us a personal sense of invisibility related to the unfolding drama of dominance (McIntosh, 1988). This invisibility was clearly illustrated in a workshop I recently led for a group of senior-level administrators at a large university in Australia. In this university the student population was highly diverse, yet the upper-level managers were exclusively White and predominantly male. From previous work with Aboriginal students, international students, and diverse members of the faculty and staff, I knew there were many issues of equity that were not being adequately addressed by senior management. I began my half-day session with a discussion of European hegemony and social dominance in educational settings. I wanted to introduce a basic conceptual framework for understanding dominance and then spend most of our time developing strategies for more equitable policies and practices. It soon became clear, however, that these senior managers did not accept my beginning premise regarding White dominance. And without acknowledging the reality of dominance, we could not engage in a discussion of strategies for change.

Swimming in White dominance, these university administrators were not able or willing to critically analyze their own social positionality. They were each highly accomplished and respected scholars and administrators in their own right, but profoundly ignorant of the dynamics of social dominance relative to their position of power within the university. I realized that my brief workshop should have been preceded by a more lengthy and remedial course on the history of intergroup relations and White social dominance in Australia.

For White educators, it is especially important that we lift the curtain of ignorance and denial that has protected us from understanding our location on the broader stage of hierarchical social arrangements. We need to see how the lives of our students have been scripted by their membership in groups differing in degrees of social dominance and marginality. In the case of the teacher in Texas, who saw all her students coming into her classroom with "the same stuff," it is clear that she, like the university administrators in Australia, had not learned the skills to adequately and critically assess her own role in the larger social drama of dominance. As James Banks (1996) reminds us:

> If we fail to recognize the ways in which social location produces subjectivity and influences the construction of knowledge, we are unlikely to interrogate established knowledge that contributes to the oppression of marginalized and victimized groups. (p. 65)

Social Dominance Theory

Social dominance theory offers a third research strand that can help inform educational practitioners who are concerned with issues of equity and social justice. The four basic assumptions of social dominance theory (Sidanius & Pratto, 1993) are the following:

1. Human social systems are predisposed to form social hierarchies, with hegemonic groups at the top and negative reference groups at the bottom.
2. Hegemonic groups tend to be disproportionately male, a phenomenon that social dominance theorist call the "iron law of andrancy."
3. Most forms of social oppression, such as racism, sexism, and classism, can be viewed as manifestations of group-based social hierarchy.
4. Social hierarchy is a survival strategy that has been selected by many species of primates, including *Homo sapiens*.

By way of definition within social dominance theory, "hegemonic groups" are those that tend to be disproportionately represented at the higher positions of authority within social institutions, whereas "negative reference groups" are those that are least likely to be represented there (Sidanius & Pratto, 1993).

Social dominance theorists take the notion of social positionality and cast it in a historical and evolutionary context of survival and immutability. There is a deterministic tone to their assumptions and conclusions regarding human social systems. Similar to the minimal group paradigm, social dominance theorists suggest that human beings are inherently predisposed to create group-based systems of categorization and discrimination. Sidanius and Pratto (1993) propose that an "oppression equilibrium" must be established to stabilize any society, wherein there is enough oppression to keep the hierarchical arrangements in place, but not so much as to cause either outright rebellion or the total destruction of negative reference groups, that is, genocide. Social hierarchies are maintained through a combination of individual and institutional discrimination, which also must be limited to prevent social destabilization and to avoid excessive conflict with the expressed values and beliefs of the social system. The most stable societies, these theorists maintain, are those in which negative reference groups accept the legitimacy of the hierarchical structure, thus internalizing their oppression by rationalizing to themselves their place in the scheme of things.

Social dominance theory builds on a functional approach to the study of individual attitudes, values, and beliefs (D. Katz, 1960). From this point of view, individuals develop belief structures that support and rationalize their social position and their collective reality. Social dominance theorists maintain that the functional role of values and beliefs applies not only to individuals but also to social systems. Thus, within hierarchical systems, most social institutions are supported by a set of "legitimizing myths" that serve to explain and rationalize the differential distribution of power and rewards in favor of the dominant group (Sidanius & Pratto, 1993). Appleby (1992) draws a similar conclusion from her analysis of the founding of the colonial system in North America:

> Being the true heirs of European culture, the American colonists had perpetuated the invidious distinction between the talented few and the vulgar many, making status an important feature of all their institutional arrangements. (p. 425)

Social dominance theorists argue that hierarchical systems of group-based preference are inevitable, immutable, and universal in human experience. In their approach to social dominance theory, Sidanius and Pratto (1993) seem more concerned with issues of social equilibrium and stability than with the achievement of equity and social justice. Because of their fixed and deterministic perspective, and in light of their pessimism regarding the possibility of change, it might be argued that social dominance theorists have actually created their own grand legitimizing myth for the perpetuation of White dominance.

Privilege and Penalty

In addition to the minimal group paradigm, social positionality, and social dominance theory, a fourth direction in the literature looks at dominance as a system of "privilege and penalty" (McIntosh, 1988; Nieto, 2005a; M. Weinberg, 1991). From this perspective, social arrangements of dominance cause privileges to flow to certain groups whether or not those privileges are earned. Likewise, penalties, punishments, and inequities flow to other groups through no fault of their own other than their group membership. Like the Iowa banker who experienced his dominance as a "fish discovering water," many of these privileges flow to Whites without our awareness or intent, and they continue to flow to us even if we consciously desire *not* to be dominant (G. Howard, 1993; McIntosh, 1988; Sleeter, 1996; Wise, 2003). The privilege-and-penalty analysis echoes in many ways the notions of hegemonic and negative reference groups in social dominance theory. Both approaches are descriptive of the actual history of interaction between dominant and subordinate groups, wherein group-based inequalities are intrinsically linked to the very foundations of personal and institutional behavior. Systems of privilege and penalty are also consistent with the minimal group paradigm, in that both conceptual frameworks are based on the dynamics of group-based categorization and discrimination.

Research Implications

Taken together, research findings in the areas of minimal group paradigm, social positionality, social dominance theory, and systems of privilege and penalty form a strong foundation for understanding White dominance. First, the minimal group paradigm suggests that all human beings are predisposed to form in-groups and out-groups and to respond to other human beings based on these self-created, and sometimes trivial, distinctions. Second, work in the area of social positionality reminds us that our place in the social hierarchy of dominance determines how we construct knowledge, how we come to determine what is real and true. Third, social dominance theory places systems of dominance and subordination in an evolutionary context, arguing that such group-based arrangements have been ever-present, and perhaps even inevitable, in human experience. Finally, work in the area of privilege and penalty demonstrates that systems of social dominance are characterized by the differential distribution of rewards and punishments to individuals not on the basis of individual worth but solely as a function of group membership.

The research literature clearly demonstrates that social dominance is a common human phenomenon, not a uniquely White issue. As I stated in the introduction to this chapter, the viper of social dominance comes in all colors. Actually, we need look no further than our daily newspaper for continual reminders of social dominance as evidenced by widely varied peoples and cultures. Realities such as the Chinese occupation of Tibet, the Japanese oppression of the Ainu in Hokkaido, the Turkish genocide against the Armenians, the Black-on-Black acts of genocide in Rwanda and Darfur, and many other ethnic power struggles around the world clearly establish that the drive for social dominance is not a peculiarly "White thing."

However, when we consider social dominance in the context of Western education, and in light of the broad-based expansion of European influence throughout the world, it is important to explore the particular nature of White dominance. Precisely because our White forebears had both the means and the will to establish cultural dominance in many corners of the world, we as White educators ought to understand how our inherited hegemonic position continues to influence the educational process today. Because European dominance has been so broadly and effectively established, it is important to ask ourselves as White educators how our own social positionality and history of dominance might be implicated in the disproportionate distribution of privilege and penalty in contemporary educational systems, which is so clearly evidenced by the persistence of a race-based achievement gap. We ought to seek this understanding not because we stand accused of the sins and excesses of our ancestors, but because we are committed to equitable opportunities and outcomes for all of our students.

In seeking this understanding, however, it must be acknowledged that it is often difficult for the members of any hegemonic group to see their own dominance. Because of our social positionality as Whites in Western settings, the arrangements of dominance may appear "normal" to us, part of the assumed and natural fabric of reality. For this reason, I have often found it difficult, as with the university administrators in Australia, to engage my White colleagues in an authentic dialogue about White dominance. This difficulty is partly a function of denial and defensiveness, but it also relates to the lack of an adequate lens for viewing our own dominance, a lens that allows us to see beyond the blinders of social positionality.

THE LENS OF INDIGENOUS EXPERIENCE

In my work with White educators I have found it helpful to use the lens of "otherness" as a vehicle for understanding dominance. Learning from the experiences of those groups who have been marginalized by White dominance has been the primary vehicle for my own growth in this arena. The opportunities that were afforded me in the Hill neighborhood in New Haven to glimpse reality through the eyes of Black children and Black community activists were pivotal in my development as an educator and as a human being (Chapter 1). These experiences led me to conclude that

White multicultural awareness must be mediated through actual engage-ment with "the other." Authentic engagement with the reality of those whose stories are significantly different from our own can allow us to transcend, to some degree, the limits of social positionality and help us see dominance in a clearer light.

In addition to the New Haven years, profound lessons about White dominance have come through my engagement with Indigenous people from many parts of the world. Through the eyes of Indigenous people, and from the perspective of their many centuries of exposure to European dominance, I have gained a deeper understanding of Whiteness in the West. In this section I will review much of the information that has come to me through the lens of Indigenous peoples' experiences in dealing with Whites throughout the past 500 years. I share these lessons here as a way of illustrating the actual methodologies of dominance, the means by which the theoretical issues explored above have become manifested in the lives of human beings. It is a painful story to tell, and I do not recount it with the intention of casting blame or inciting guilt. I choose to enter this discussion here because it is important that we understand White dominance in more than a theoretical way. If we are to grow in our effectiveness as White edu-cators of diverse students, we need to understand how theories such as the minimal group paradigm, social positionality, social dominance, and privilege and penalty actually influence the lives of children and the out-comes of education. For me, the lens of Indigenous experience has given a human face to these theoretical constructs.

The Methodologies of Dominance

I share my thoughts here from the perspective of a "non-Indigenous" person who has attended a series of four World Indigenous People's Conferences on Education. The first was held in Vancouver, Canada, in 1987, hosted by Native Canadians; the second in Ngaruawahia, New Zealand, in 1990, hosted by the Maori people; the third in Wollongong, New South Wales, in 1993, hosted by the Aboriginal people of Australia; and the fourth in Albuquerque, New Mexico, in 1996, hosted by Native Americans.

Although these Indigenous meetings, which continue to occur every three years, have received little attention in the global press, I feel they are one of the more significant educational phenomena occurring in the present era of school reform. The conferences have drawn delegates from widely diverse cultures, with more than 5,000 people from 28 countries attending the Australian event. The many Indigenous nations, tribes, and cultural groups who are drawn to these conferences share a common historical experience: They all played host to Europe's "Age of Discovery." The conferences themselves have been a vehicle for acknowledging the common suffering of the colonial experience and a means for coalescing the power and vision of colonized people. For the first time in history, Indigenous people from all parts of the planet, people who have heretofore suffered separately from the overlay of White dominance, are now coming together to share their stories, seek healing, preserve their cultures, and secure political empowerment. The conferences are also an attempt to assure that the oppression, pain, and racism of the past 500 years are not continued in the future. In this way, the World Indigenous People's Conferences are attempting to shift the tide of global history by unraveling the legacy of Western domination.

The Mapuche of Chile, the Maya of Mexico, the Cherokee of the United States, the Mohawk of Canada, the Native People of Hawai'i, the Cordillera people of the Philippines, the Aboriginal people of Australia, the Maori of New Zealand, the Masai of Kenya, and the many other groups who have attended these conferences all have similar stories to share. For each of these groups of people, being "discovered" by Europeans has resulted in devastating loss and oppression through the combination of disease, warfare, land theft, discriminatory government policy, the removal of children from their homes, the introduction of alcohol, and the use of foreign religion and education as tools of forced assimilation and cultural genocide. The methods used by Westerners to colonize each of the various groups of Indigenous people are so similar that each group immediately recognizes its own experience in the stories of the others. The striking similarity in the processes employed by Europeans in establishing dominance has led me to ponder whether some obscure fifteenth-century bureaucrat may have authored a handbook entitled, "The Seven Basics of Western Dominance: Bacteria, Bullets, Beads, Bureaucracy, Books, Booze, and the Bible."

I will describe briefly how these various elements in the methodology of dominance have influenced the lives of Indigenous people and cemented the foundation of Western dominance in lands throughout the world. The discussion that follows is intended to illustrate the actual workings of White dominance in the lives of people who have been its victims and to help us see more clearly the implications of the theoretical issues explored in the previous section. Except where otherwise noted, I base my account on information shared with me by delegates to the World Indigenous People's Conferences on Education.

Disease. Bacteria were usually the primary killer of Indigenous people who were unfortunate enough to be on the receiving end of European expansion. Within the first century of White contact in North America, for example, European diseases had devastated up to 90% of the population in some of the Eastern Algonquin Nations, and by 1837 the entire Mandan Nation on the banks of the Missouri River had been reduced by smallpox to only 37 survivors (Lewis, 1996). European diseases spread so fast among American Indian Nations that one-half of the Nez Perce´ people had died of smallpox a full-quarter century before the first White person was seen in Nez Perce´ country (Ward, 1996). In some cases European bacteria were used as weapons of war through the intentional distribution of smallpox-infested blankets to Native people who stood in the path of Manifest Destiny (Prucha, 1975). The great irony of this tragic period is that American Indian people had no similarly devastating bacteria to pass on to the Europeans.

Warfare. Violence was often used to eliminate those Indigenous people who did not fall victim to European diseases. In Central America and Mexico, as a result of Spanish invasion, violence, and accompanying diseases, over two-thirds of the Indian population were killed between 1519 and 1650 (Jonas, 1991). In the United States, General William Tecumseh Sherman was anxious after the Civil War to find some basis to justify a major war with the Indians. Viewing them as "the enemies of our race and our civilization," he said in 1866, "God only knows when, and I do not see how, we can make a decent excuse for an Indian War" (cited in Lewis, 1996, p. 386).

Similarly, several of my Aboriginal colleagues in Australia share accounts of the mass organized killing of Aboriginal people carried out by European invaders in their attempt to "clear" the land for grazing and White settlement. To this end, many young men who were anxious for adventure and new opportunity in the land down under were recruited out of Wales, Scotland, and other countries to come to Australia as "shooters." Ostensibly hired to kill predatory animals, many did not know until they arrived in Australia that their targets would be human (Bob Morgan, personal communication, June 1994). Upon learning the truth, some refused to carry out their assigned mission. An Aboriginal friend, for example, told me that his grandfather originally came from Wales as a shooter, but when he discovered the evil for which he had been hired, he abandoned his employers, married an Aboriginal woman, and lived out the rest of his life among her family and community.

Land Theft. The imposition of European notions of private ownership and the appropriation of Native land are perennial topics of discussion at the World Indigenous People's Conferences. In their early contact with Whites, most Indigenous people were astonished by the strange European proclivity for buying and selling pieces of the earth. As expressed by Chief Joseph (Hin-mah-too-yah-lat-kekht) of the Nez Perce´, the Indigenous view of the land was much different:

> The earth was created by the assistance of the sun, and it should be left as it was. . . . The country was made without lines of demarcation, and it is no man's business to divide it. . . . I see the Whites all over the country gaining wealth, and I see their desire to give us lands which are worthless. . . . The earth and myself are of one mind. The measure of the land and the measure of our bodies are the same. (cited in McLuhan, 1971, p. 28)

Chief Joseph's sentiments are not an artifact of the past, and it is often difficult for Westerners today to comprehend the power and centrality of Indigenous people's continuing connection to the land. Aboriginal elders, for example, are often personally responsible for particular sacred sites in Australia. From generation to generation, specific caretaker roles are passed on, requiring an individual to watch over an important place or feature of the land, to keep its stories and its songs, and to be a protector of that location (Lorraine Mafi-Williams, personal communication, January 1991). If these places are desecrated through mining or other forms of economic development, the Aboriginal caretakers may be so disturbed by the violation of the land that they themselves will die along with the spirit of the land they were pledged to defend (Erica Hampton, personal communication, January 1991). This Aboriginal view of the land has always stood in stark contrast to the utilitarian view of the early British settlers, as evidenced by Sir Thomas Mitchell's (1839) refections upon his "discovery" of the plains of Western Victoria:

> The scene was different from anything I had ever before witnessed, either in New South Wales or elsewhere, a land so inviting yet without inhabitants. As I stood, the first intruder on the sublime solitude of these verdant plains as yet untouched by flocks of herds, I felt conscious of being the harbinger of mighty changes, and that our steps would soon be followed by the men and animals for whom it seemed to have been prepared. (p. 159)

Indigenous people on many continents today are waging continuing political battles to protect, recover, and preserve their lands from the kind of proprietary hubris expressed by Mitchell (Solidarity Foundation, 1996; B. Weinberg, 1996). In Guatemala, for example, it was not until 1996 that the Mayan people were able to return from exile in Mexico to reclaim homelands taken from them in a 1954 CIA-sponsored coup that opened their land for take-over by the U.S.-based United Fruit Company (Jonas, 1991). In another case, a participant I met at the 1993 conference in Australia wrote in a recent letter to me that his people are facing "torture, rape, extrajudicial execution, arbitrary arrest, and disappearances" because of their efforts to protect their land and preserve their culture. For his protection I choose not to identify his specific Indigenous group, but my friend speaks for many peoples of the world who are suffering today from the continuing encroachment of Western dominance.

In the United States, of course, we have a long tradition of taking Native land, even that which was once guaranteed by treaty to remain in American Indian hands "for as long as the rivers shall run" (Deloria, 1974). President Andrew Jackson, chief architect of the "Trail of Tears," justified one such program of theft, the Indian Removal Act of 1830, with the following words:

> These tribes cannot exist surrounded by our settlements and continual contact with our citizens. They have neither the intelligence, the industry, the moral habits, nor the desire of improvement. They must necessarily yield to the force of circumstance and, ere long, disappear. (cited in Ward, 1996, p. 83)

Having once accomplished, through Jackson's policies, the task of removing most of the American Indians east of the Mississippi, a young nation hungry for land then proceeded to take the American West as well. The "legitimizing myth" for this relentless acquisition of American Indian land was well articulated in 1843 by Missouri Congressman Thomas Hart Benton: "The White race went for the land and they will continue to go for it. . . . the principle is founded in God's command and it will continue to be obeyed" (*Congressional Globe*, 1846, pp. 917–918).

For comparative purposes, it is interesting to look at the process of land appropriation in Australia. By the time the British began to invade Australia in 1788, they had learned many lessons in America. According to the doctrine of discovery, which had been established in Europe by the early 1500s, if explorers of new lands found people living there, they could not claim those lands directly for their home countries (Williams, 1990). They could legitimately claim only the right to negotiate for the land with its prior inhabitants. The doctrine of discovery was the foundation for the entire treaty-making process in the Americas, forcing European nations to acknowledge, however ingenuously, the legitimacy of Native title.

Having found the doctrine of discovery to be a cumbersome and inefficient process in the Americas, necessitating the continual making and breaking of treaties and the constant creation of justifications for illegal practices, the British in Australia decided to avoid the entire ordeal. They did so by declaring Australia *terra nullius,* which means "empty land," land without human occupants. In this way the British established a "legal" justification for taking the entire continent. They then proceeded to bring *terra nullius* into reality by disposing with treaties and going directly to bullets, thus enacting a program of genocide that would leave many Aboriginal language groups extinct by the twentieth century (Broome, 1982). It was not until 1993, following the Australian High Court decision in the landmark *Mabo* case, that the Australian Parliament finally recognized the legitimacy of Native title (*Mabo v. Queensland*, No. 2, 1992).

Religion. In addition to the devastating loss of life and land, the use of the Bible and Christianity as tools of oppression has been a particularly sad chapter in the establishment of White dominance. In the early 1500s, while Europeans were launching their frenzy of discovery and encountering new lands and cultures around the world, there was a major debate among the Christian hierarchy in Europe regarding the spiritual status of Indigenous people (Williams, 1990). Since these people were not Christians, they were seen by Europeans as "infidels." The central question of church debate became, "Are the infidels human?" If Indigenous people were not fully human, then by church doctrine they did not possess souls and could not be converted to Christianity. If, however, they were determined to be human, it would become the church's obligation to bring their souls into the "one true faith." This debate was carried on as part of the discussion regarding the doctrine of discovery, wherein European nations considered possible justifications for claiming new lands and depriving the original inhabitants of life, liberty, and property (Williams, 1990).

Ultimately, of course, the existence of Indigenous souls was decided in the affirmative by the White church fathers, opening the way for Christianity to play a key role in the expansion of European hegemony. The Age of Discovery was thereby granted a holy mission—not only to claim new real estate for the nobles back home but also to bring the "heathens" to Jesus. Those Indigenous people who had not fallen victim to European bacteria or bullets would now be subjected to the invaders' view of spiritual truth. Many Indigenous leaders foresaw what was coming, as is clear in these words of warning delivered by Sweet Medicine to his fellow Cheyenne prior to White encroachment on their land:

> Some day you will meet a people who are White. They will try to give you many things, but do not take them. At last, I think you will take these things and they will bring sickness to you. . . . Your ways will change. You will leave your religion for something new. You will lose respect for your leaders and start quarrelling with one another. . . . You will take the new ways and forget the good things by which you have lived and in the end you will become worse than crazy. (cited in Ward, 1996, p. 30)

In most countries invaded by Europeans, missionaries became the advanced guard for the "civilizing" process. Good Christians made compliant subjects. Traditional Indigenous spiritual practices were made illegal, and people who chose to continue practicing them were punished and/or forced to go underground. The Makah, for example, who are a whaling people on the northwestern tip of Washington State, would canoe across the treacherous waters off Cape Flattery to Tatoosh Island, where they could celebrate their longhouse traditions out of sight of their White overseers, who were afraid to venture across the rough seas. Changes in the policies of spiritual repression have been slow in coming. In the United States, it was not until 1978 (Harvey & Harjo, 1994) that Congress finally passed the Indian Religious Freedom Act, and even today some groups of traditional practitioners, such as the Native American Church, are continually harassed.

Missionaries and Bureaucrats. The oversight and administration of Indigenous communities in the United States and Australia were often delegated to missionaries (Reyhner & Eder, 1989). Governments in both countries parceled out communities of Indigenous people to different Christian denominations. As part of the "peace policy" in the United States, the Catholics, Baptists, Lutherans, Congregationalists, Anglicans, Dutch Reform, and most other major Christian bodies received an allocation of Indigenous souls to place under the care of their particular doctrine. In his annual report of 1872, the Commissioner of Indian Affairs, Francis A. Walker, spoke highly of this "extra-official" relationship between the U.S. government and the churches, and he summoned the missionaries "to assume charge of the intellectual and moral education of the Indians" (cited in Prucha, 1975, p. 142).

Enormous power was given to these "mission managers," as they came to be called in Australia (Rowley, 1970). The Christian overseers were responsible for the distribution of food rations, the allocation of jobs, and the granting of permission to travel off the mission or the reservation. These faith-based bureaucrats administered a system of privilege and penalty designed for the control and compliance of Native people. Conversion to Christianity was often a necessary survival strategy for Indigenous people who wished to feed, clothe, and house their families (Fuchs & Havinghurst, 1973). Thus the Bible joined with the bureaucracy in the paternalistic control of Indigenous people's lives.

Education. The removal of Indigenous children from their homes to attend boarding schools is one of the most tragic stories in the history of White dominance. Education was often used as a tool for reinforcing the colonial policies of forced assimilation (Robinson-Zañartu, 1996, 2003). In the United States, American Indian children were usually taken so far from their parents that they would not be able to run home. Administered under the euphemistic intention of "civilizing the Indian," the boarding schools were, in fact, a severe system of cultural genocide (Reyhner & Eder, 1989). Evincing both the misguided idealism and the blind racism of the boarding school policy, the Commissioner of Indian Affairs in 1889 laid out the following "principles for Indian education":

> Education is to be the medium through which the rising generation of Indians are to be brought into fraternal and harmonious relationship with their white fellow-citizens, and with them enjoy the sweets of refined homes, the delights of social intercourse, the emoluments of commerce and trade, the advantages of travel, together with the pleasures that come from literature, science and philosophy, and the solace and stimulus afforded by a true religion. (cited in Prucha, 1975, p. 178)

In spite of this flowery pronouncement, neither delight nor pleasure came to American Indian people as a result of the boarding school policy. Children were removed from their families at a young age and kept for many years. Their hair was cut in Western style. Traditional clothing, ornamentation, spirituality, and language were forbidden. Punishments for violation of rules in the boarding schools were harsh, painful, and humiliating (Robinson et al., 2004). Christian indoctrination was an integral part of the process of deculturalizing Native children, an attempt to "bring the infidels and savages living in those parts to human civility" (Vogel, 1972, pp. 45–46). The stated intention of the policy was to "kill the Indian . . . and save the man" (O'Brien, 1889, cited in Harvey & Harjo, 1994, p. 134). The "educational" value of these schools was limited, with the curriculum being primarily geared to training for menial labor and domestic servitude.

Similar policies were instituted in Australia, creating a "stolen generation" of Aboriginal children who did not have the benefit of growing up in their own families and communities (Reed, 1982). An Aboriginal friend shared with me her memories of being taken from her parents at the age of 12, never to see them again until she was 21 years old. The officers of the "Aboriginal Protection Board" came into the homes of her friends and neighbors on the mission and forcibly removed children from their parents. As in the United States, these Aboriginal children were often taken to boarding schools where they would receive Christian indoctrination and training as domestic workers. My friend spent many years as a menial laborer in White homes before she was finally able in her late forties to demonstrate her considerable academic and intellectual skills by completing a university degree and becoming a noted writer and filmmaker. It would be impossible to adequately describe or quantify the extent to which the intellectual and creative potential of young Indigenous students has been either derailed or destroyed through the coercive assimilation of the boarding school policies in both Australia and the United States (Dupris, 1979; Robinson-Zañartu, 2003). For purposes of classroom discussion of this process, the Australian film, *Rabbit-Proof Fence* (Phillip Noyce, Miramax, 2002), is an excellent and historically accurate resource. [1]

Alienation and Alcohol. The tragic impact of education as a tool for forced assimilation continues into the present. Even into the late 1960s, American Indian students at boarding schools were being coerced into religious training, with various Christian denominations given direct access to captive audiences of Indigenous children (Carlson, 1997). The ongoing process of humiliation and deculturalization is in the memory of American Indian people living today. Those who experienced years of mistreatment in the boarding schools often returned to their families as broken and lost individuals (Locust, 1988). Forced assimilation left them too White to be accepted by their relatives back on the reservation, and yet they remained too Indian to be accepted into White society. Many turned to alcohol to ease the pain of their alienation from their own identity (Emerson, 1997; Yates, 1987). A Turtle Mountain Cree colleague, Ken LaFountaine, who has created a program at Shoreline Community College in Washington State for educating White students about Indian history, attributes a major portion of American Indian alcoholism and suicide today to the continuing and devastating effects of the boarding school policy.

Dominance Continues

Even today it is difficult for many non-Indian teachers to work effectively with American Indian students (Deloria, 1991; McDermott, cited in Moll, 1991; Robinson et al., 2004). This was made clear to me in the 1980s when the rural school district where I taught received a new influx of Indian families. The Stillaguamish tribe won federal recognition and reclamation of traditional lands in our community, and in the course of one year Indian students became a significant new presence in our classrooms. Almost immediately upon their arrival, however, teachers began complaining that these students "didn't fit in well" and that Indian parents "showed little interest in their children's education."

---

1. Based on the book, *Follow the Rabbit-Proof Fence,* by Doris Pilkington and Nugi Garimara

Many of my colleagues didn't realize that the trauma of the boarding school experience is a very present memory for the parents and the grandparents of today's American Indian students, often creating considerable tension and cultural discontinuity between the home and the school (Joe, 1994; Secada, 1991). Although most Indian families want the same positive educational outcomes for their children as other parents do, the emotional legacy of cultural genocide is not easily overcome. For generations of Indian people, schooling has not been a positive experience, and it will take much work on the part of educators to regain their trust.

This trust was not easily developed in my local school district. Most of our teachers, like their peers nationwide, had little experience or understanding of the culture and learning characteristics of Indigenous children (Havinghurst, 1978; Reynolds, 2005). From their social positionality of Whiteness, teachers described Indian students as "withdrawn, shy, quiet, inattentive, and unmotivated." Consequently, our school psychologist soon became overwhelmed with teacher requests for special education testing of Indian students. According to teachers and other White workers in the schools, these students were "unresponsive" in the classrooms, "causing problems" on the playground, truant at the high school, and receiving inordinate numbers of discipline tickets on the school buses. Ironically, the same students described by teachers as being passive and withdrawn in the classrooms were accused by others of being aggressive and obnoxious outside the classroom. Indian students were being viewed as a negative reference group within the school culture, and school district personnel were imposing diagnostic assumptions based on the legitimizing myths underlying their position of social dominance.

Teacher misperceptions and assumptions about Indian students in our school district reflected a broad national trend that places Indian students as a group at the highest risk of school failure, dropping out, and overrepresentation in special education (Hebbeler et al., 2001; McShane, 1983; Robinson-Zañartu, 2003; Yates, 1987). Realizing that the actual deficiency lay more with us as educators than with either American Indian students or their families, my wife, Lotus Linton, and I launched an educational program for teachers and other employees, which we called "The Indian Child in the Classroom." Experts in the field of Indian education, who were also members of various Indian communities in our state, came to share their perspectives and strategies with our faculty and staff. Participants gained an Indian historical perspective, an understanding of the long-lasting effects of dominance, and an introduction to features of Indian culture that related directly to their work with American Indian students. Indian parents were pleased that the school district cared enough to provide this education for the teachers and staff. The process resulted in considerable change in the school district. We didn't solve all the problems that have evolved over centuries of dominance and cultural conflict, but we did manage to shift the focus away from blaming the Indian students and their parents. Working together, we gradually began to take mutual responsibility for creating a more positive educational environment for American Indian children.

WHITE DOMINANCE IN THEORY AND PRACTICE

The experience of Indigenous people relative to European expansion over the past 500 years graphically demonstrates the methodologies of White dominance. Through the lens of Indigenous experience, the theoretical issues of dominance discussed earlier can be viewed in the living context of the past and the present. Consistent with research findings related to the minimal group paradigm, Native peoples throughout the world have been categorized as "the other." From the perspective of the European invaders, Indigenousness, in itself, became a powerful marker for defining the "we" and the "they" of the colonial experience, creating a basis for discrimination against an out-group that the Europeans had defined as inferior. As would be predicted by the theory of social positionality, European colonialists constructed social reality through education, religion, and government policy in such a way as to justify and perpetuate their position of power. Consistent with social dominance theory, Whites in the colonialized world established a set of legitimizing myths that characterized Indigenous people as infidels, heathens, savages, and uncivilized, thus deepening the divide of social positionality between themselves and those whom they had designated as a negative reference group. And finally, White hegemony soon became embedded in systems of privilege and penalty that further legitimized and exacerbated the subordinate position of Indigenous people.

It is clear from the brief review of Indigenous experience presented in this chapter that the methodologies of dominance have been intentional, targeted, consistent across diverse and distant settings, and highly effective in establishing White social hegemony. It is also clear, as I discovered in my own school district, that White dominance is not a relic of the past but continues to have direct and deleterious influence in the lives of children today. It is also important to point out that many marginalized groups have experienced White dominance in ways similar to Indigenous people.

Carlson (1997), who has studied American Indian boarding schools in the 1960s and inner-city predominantly Black and Hispanic schools in the 1990s, has concluded that similar elements of colonialism are present in both. He reminds us that we cannot improve the quality of education for any group of racial and cultural "others" in Western nations today without first understanding the extent to which our educational practices and institutions continue to be influenced by colonial beliefs and power relations. Kozol's (1991, 2005) work in inner-city schools, such as those in East St. Louis, where he witnessed Black children living and attending school under abominable conditions, documents similar conclusions. Also, Todorov (1982) discovered from his extensive study of the colonial process that "it is in fact the conquest of America that heralds and establishes our present identity" (p. 5). And if we want to work seriously on the issues of inequality for Blacks and other oppressed people, West (1993a) reminds us that we must begin not with the "problems" of marginalized groups but with the fundamental social flaws that have been created by White dominance.

The lens of Indigenous experience provides one vehicle for helping White educators see the consequences of social dominance. Through the eyes of the "other" we are able to penetrate the barrier of social positionality and see ourselves from a more realistic perspective. When we expand the focal point to include other marginalized groups, it becomes clear that the shadow of dominance is not merely a theoretical construct but a living reality that continues to occlude the clear light of opportunity for many of our students today.

THE POSSIBILITY OF CHANGE

Once again, it must be emphasized that the exploration of White dominance presented above is not intended to incite blame, shame, or guilt on the part of White educators. As I stated at the beginning of this chapter, the beast of dominance comes in many colors and guises, and Whites alone do not hold a monopoly on the imposition of human suffering. I have engaged the issue of White dominance here because it has had such a broad impact throughout the world. It is not the only form of dominance, but it has been the most pervasive in Western educational settings. Also, I have recognized in my 40 years of multicultural education work that many White educators, like fish immersed in the normalcy of water, have been swimming unaware in the medium of our own dominance. Only when we begin to see ourselves through a different lens, as we did through the perspective of Indigenous people above, does the image of our social position come more clearly into focus.

The literature on social dominance suggests that human beings are predisposed for the formation of group-based hierarchies. We tend to draw distinctions between in-groups and out-groups and quite naturally come to discriminate in favor of our own group. When power is added to the formula, hegemonic groups are able to construct reality in ways that both perpetuate and justify their social position. Social dominance theorists claim that these arrangements of social control are immutable and evolutionarily determined. Whether or not we agree with their pessimistic assessment, it is clear that White dominance has had tremendous staying power in those nations that have been affected by European expansion.

I am hopeful that White educators in multicultural schools can come to see the broader context of our work and begin to understand the significant and varying impact of dominance in the lives of the students we serve. It is from this perspective that we can finally approach the teacher in Texas who was mystified by her observation of differential student outcomes based on race and culture. Our children, as we have seen so clearly through the lens of Indigenous experience, do *not* come to us with "the same stuff." Many of the negative influences of history have been disproportionately distributed across the lives of our students, and these "savage inequalities" remain with us today (Kozol, 1991).

Neither the pains nor the privileges of history have been allocated fairly in the lives of children. The realities of group membership in terms of race, culture, language, economics, and social positionality are inextricably tied to educational outcomes. Like the teachers of American Indian students in my school district, we too often attribute failure to the culture and characteristics of the child rather than to the inherent structure of dominance in the larger society. In our lack of awareness we can become mere pawns of dominance, perpetuating the legitimizing myths that have kept Whites in control for centuries. If we do not understand dominance, we cannot hope to transcend it.

I believe that most White educators want schooling to become more than a mechanism of social control that favors White children. Those of us who share this conviction must choose to become more aware—to open our eyes, our minds, and our hearts to the realities of dominance. In making this choice, we are challenged to embark on a great journey. It is a difficult journey down a river of healing, through many whitewater rapids and the often treacherous currents of self-examination and personal change (see Chapters 5 and 6). In accepting this challenge, we are called to transform both ourselves and the social arrangements of positionality and dominance that have favored us as White people. The tide of our own past history is against us on this journey, but the force of the river and the future of our students require that we join the quest. As a participant in one of my recent multicultural workshops stated, "We are a world in need of healing, but healing can begin only when we acknowledge the depth of our pain."

Too much human energy has already been expended in perpetuating the cycles of pain, dominance, submission, blame, guilt, and denial. We have danced around the edges of democracy for two centuries, but rarely have we committed ourselves to realize its deepest vision of justice and liberty. We have talked incessantly about racial inequality, but seldom have we engaged the conversation around healing and reconciliation. In the chapters that follow I will consider how we might attempt to bring education, social reality, and our own thoughts and actions into closer alignment with our expressed values of pluralistic community. If we can face the painful truths of White dominance, and not fall victim to the enervating cycles of blame and guilt, there is some hope that we might then be able to engage our hearts and our hands in the healing work of social transformation.

CHAPTER 3

Decoding the Dominance Paradigm

> I consider the fundamental theme of our epoch to be domina-
> tion—which implies its opposite, the theme of liberation, as the
> objective to be achieved.
> —Paulo Freire, *Pedagogy of the Oppressed*

In the previous chapter, I described the methodologies of dominance whereby Europeans established White hegemony throughout many parts of the world. As educators committed to social transformation and healing, however, it is essential that we go further in our understanding of dominance than mere description of its more blatant manifestations. Many of the obvious and overt methodologies of dominance have now been limited by legislative and legal constraints, yet we know that the residual effects of White hegemony continue to exert a powerful downward and deleterious pull in the lives of our students who have not been marked with the racial code of privilege.

White dominance continues to weigh in as a powerful contender in the educational process, with or without the presence of blatant White supremacists. Despite decades of civil rights activity, it is the subtle and often invisible nature of White dominance that has proven to be so resistant to change in Western nations. The challenge now facing us in education is to dismantle the deeper nature of racism and dominance, a challenge that will require a more rigorous analysis of the underlying dynamics of dominance than we as White educators have yet achieved. This deeper analysis of dominance is the focus of the present chapter, and it is a task we must complete before we can realistically hope to contribute to the process of social transformation and healing.

THE DYNAMICS OF DOMINANCE

We cannot fully understand dominance without exploring the process of knowledge construction, which is the means by which individuals and societies determine what is real and true. Knowledge is never neutral (Banks, 1996; Apple et al., 2003). Our "knowing" does not necessarily describe what is real in an objective sense, but rather what is *considered* to be real in a subjective sense (Code, 1991; Fiske, 1989). "Official knowledge" is constructed by those who occupy the seats of power in all major social institutions, including education (Apple, 2000). Personal truth may be in the mind of the beholder (a function of individual perception), but official truth is in the hands of the powerful (a function of group control). Hegemonic groups tend to construct reality in ways that reinforce, protect, and legitimize their position of dominance (Sidanius & Pratto, 1993).

Since the process of education is primarily concerned with the communication of meaning and truth, it has always been imperative, from a hegemonic group perspective, that all elements of schooling be aligned with official knowledge. In this way, the educational process has allowed those in power to selectively control the flow of knowledge and inculcate into young minds only those "truths" that solidify and perpetuate their own hegemony (Gramsci, 1972). As J. A. Banks (1997) has stated, "citizenship education in the United States has historically reinforced dominant-group hegemony" (p. 4). To break through this dam of dominance, we must begin to identify and dislodge the various building blocks from which it has been constructed. In my efforts over the past 40 years to understand how social reality has been fashioned to favor Whites, I have identified three major processes that function together as the dynamics of dominance: the assumption of rightness, the luxury of ignorance, and the legacy of privilege. I will explore each of these in the following discussion.

The Assumption of Rightness

Dominant groups tend to claim truth as their private domain. For the most part, hegemonic groups do not consider their beliefs, attitudes, and actions to be determined by cultural conditioning or the influences of group membership. As Whites, we usually don't even think of ourselves as having culture; we're simply "right." Dominant groups don't hold "perspectives," they hold "Truth." This assumption of rightness has been a powerful force in the establishment of White dominance.

In the American experience, for example, the assumption of rightness was strongly reinforced by the sense of "exceptionality" that fired the imaginations of the Founders, a belief in the "monolithic myth of American success" (Appleby, 1992, p. 427). There was a sense of perfectionism in the Founders' experiment with democracy, a conviction that they were embarking on an adventure never before experienced by humankind. The language of "inalienable rights" and "equality and justice for all" grew out of a tremendous optimism that they actually could create a new and better social arrangement than had been available in Europe.

In their revolution against England, the Founders felt they had defeated a system of hereditary superiority based on class and created a new society founded on equality. In actuality, of course, they had merely substituted a different hegemonic system, one based on race and gender as well as economic position. This American version of dominance was embedded in fact that the full rights of citizenship, for the most part, were afforded only to those who were wealthy, White, and male. The new nation, founded on the principles of equality and justice, was in fact administered under the realities of racism, sexism, and elitism (Franklin, 1976; Zinn, 2003).

The extermination of American Indians, the enslavement of Blacks, the theft of land from Mexico, and the later exploitation and marginalization of Asian American laborers did not fit well with the expressed image of the United States as a just and fair nation. A certain cognitive and moral dissonance grew as events in our history made it clear that the "pursuit of happiness" was intended for Whites only. As the dissonance intensified, there developed a need to rationalize the obvious inequalities, a way to explain the injustices, and yet keep the myth of justice alive. This need was met through an evolving sense of White superiority and Anglo-conformity (Cole & Cole, 1954).

Even the Founders had at least a nascent sense of racial superiority (Franklin, 1976). Benjamin Franklin, for instance, talked about "scouring our planet" of its darker-hued people and creating the new nation as an Anglo-Saxon haven populated by the "principal body of White people on the face of the earth" (cited in Levine, 1996, p. 108). With the emergence of "scientific" race theories "explaining" the innate and hereditary inferiority of non-European groups, the notion of White superiority was firmly in place by the middle of the nineteenth century. Horsman (1981) writes:

> By 1850, a clear pattern was emerging. From their own successful past as Puritan colonists, Revolutionary patriots, conquerors of the wilderness, and creators of an immense material prosperity, the Americans had evidence plain before them that they were a chosen people; from the English they had learned that the Anglo-Saxons had always been peculiarly gifted in the arts of government; from the scientists and ethnologists they were learning that they were of a distinct Caucasian race, innately endowed with abilities that placed them above other races; from the philologist, often through literary sources, they were learning that they were the descendants of those Aryans who followed the sun to carry civilization to the whole world. (p. 5)

With a preponderance of "evidence" thus mounting in favor of White superiority, the young nation finally found a way to justify the unequal treatment of non-White groups. Since these groups were held to be, by their very nature, innately and racially inferior, it was reasonable to remove them from the line of progress and exclude them from the benefits of equality and justice. Consistent with the assumptions of social dominance theory, a set of legitimizing myths thus began to emerge to rationalize and perpetuate White hegemony in the United States.

The ultimate legitimizing myth became that of racism itself (Montagu, 1942/1997). Racist notions about Africans, for example, became "the means of explaining slavery to people whose terrain was a republic founded on radical doctrines of liberty and natural rights" (Fields, 1990, p. 114). Formulated in the early race theories of the nineteenth century (Chase, 1977; Horsman, 1981), reinforced in the pseudoscience of eugenics in the 1920s and 1930s (Gould, 1981; Horsman, 1981; Kelves, 1985), and reincarnated yet again in the 1990s with the publication of the *The Bell Curve* (Herrnstein & Murray, 1994), the curse of racism has always been available, in both its ridiculous and its increasingly sophisticated forms, to provide a convenient rationale for White dominance.

Racism for Whites has been like a crazy uncle who has been locked away for generations in the hidden attic of our collective social reality. This old relative has been part of the family for a long time. Everyone knows he's living with us, because we bring him food and water occasionally, but nobody wants to take him out in public. He is an embarrassment and a pain to deal with, yet our little family secret is that he is rich and the rest of us are living, either consciously or unconsciously, off the wealth and power he accumulated in his heydey. Even though many of us may disapprove of the tactics he used to gain his fortune, few of us want to be written out of his will. The legacy of racism, which has been fueled and legitimized by our assumption of rightness, has haunted the house of collective White identity for centuries. How we deal with this specter is a topic I will approach in more depth in the discussion of White racial identity formation in Chapters 5 and 6.

In addition to racism and theories of White supremacy, two additional elements of the White assumption of rightness warrant comment here: the idea of the melting pot and the notion of colorblindness. The melting pot idea was immortalized in a play written in 1908 by Israel Zangwill, a Jewish immigrant who came to the United States from England. His vision of the melting pot idealized the Americanization process whereby new immigrants could "melt away" their distinctive differences and emerge in the image of Anglo-conformity. This notion was expressed in visual and physical form by the Ford Motor Company in their "Ford English School" graduation ceremonies held from 1914 to 1921 (Levine, 1996). During these celebrated public events, recently arrived immigrant workers, having completed their company-sponsored course of study in English language and American culture, would enter a huge cauldron dressed in the costume of their homeland and emerge in their best American clothes, carrying American flags.

As romantic as this image might appear from a Eurocentric perspective, the melting pot has never been a viable option for people of color. Blacks, Indians, Hispanics, and Asians, even when they wanted to assimilate, have always found the color of their skin to be a more powerful marker than any costume or flag. This reality seems difficult to grasp for many of the White educators I encounter in my work throughout the United States and Australia. They ask: "Why can't everyone just be Americans, or just Australians? Why do some people insist on 'hyphenated' names, like African American or Asian American or Aboriginal Australian? My family gave up the past, why can't yours?" In an extreme articulation of the melting pot theory, a White Australian once told me, "The problem with Aboriginal people is that they want to keep their culture." Belief in the melting pot is intimately related to the assumption of rightness: "If White folks melted, anyone can. If you haven't melted yet, you ought to."

The belief in colorblindness is a close cousin to the idea of the melting pot. In my work with White educators, I often hear the following line of reasoning: "I was raised not to see color. I have always treated everyone the same. I see people as individuals, not as member of a racial group." Similar to the melting pot idea, the declaration of colorblindness assumes that we can erase our racial categories, ignore differences, and thereby achieve an illusory state of sameness or equality. The colorblind perspective treats race as an irrelevant, invisible, and taboo topic (Rist, 1974; Schofield, 2000). The proponents of colorblindness assume that the mere perception of difference is a problem. "If I see race, I must be a racist. If I don't see color, or other differences, they will go away." For these people, the mere existence of the difference causes discomfort and must be ignored or denied. Of course, the underlying assumption is that human difference in itself is a problem.

Colorblindness grows from a dominance-oriented perspective. Difference threatens dominance, because it upsets the belief in one's own rightness. "We are all the same" translates as "We are all like me," which is comforting for those who are accustomed to dominance. A White teacher once told me that "God is colorblind," which raised the assumption of rightness to a higher level. I responded, "If God is colorblind, why did she create such a beautiful array of skin tones among the human family?" This produced a blank stare from the teacher, so I turned to my African

American colleague and asked, "Jessie, if I tell you I don't see your color, how does that make you feel?" His response was, "You don't see me." That led to tears from the teacher. Her claim to colorblindness was coming from the goodness of her heart. Her assumption of rightness was well intended, as it often is. It was painful for her to realize that her dearly held belief in the sameness of human beings actually denied the authentic existence of people whose experiences of reality were different from hers. Dominance dies a difficult death, for individuals as well as nations.

The Roots of Rightness

Because the assumption of rightness has been deeply imbedded in White social reality, it is important to consider the source of this propensity for so narrowly circumscribing the parameters of truth. What has fueled White society's need to impose a single set of assumptions on people as diverse as Aboriginal Australians, American Indians, Africans, Pacific Islanders, and many other groups around the globe? In my efforts to uncover the central beliefs that have supported the hubris of Western dominance, I have found that the deepest legitimizing myths lie at the core of our theology and religion. Even though Christianity has for centuries inspired great acts of compassion and social justice, the temporal power of the Christian church has also at times been subverted to serve the purposes of White social dominance. In the analysis that follows I seek not to disparage the essential message of the Christian tradition but merely to elucidate the unfortunate means whereby the politics of greed and racism can sometimes misdirect the power of even our most sacred institutions.

Judeo-Christian legends of creation place man, and later woman, in a garden over which they are given dominion. "And God blessed them, and God said unto them, 'Be fruitful, and multiply, and replenish the earth, and subdue it: and have dominion over the fish of the sea, and over the fowl of the air, and over every living thing that moveth upon the earth'" (Genesis 1:28). First, from the beginning of time, those societies that draw on the cosmology of the Old Testament have been predisposed, by order of their God, to establish dominance. Second, it was not all human beings who were granted this divine trust, but only those who were within the fold of Judaism, and later Christianity. Thus, the notion of the "chosen people," which is a central tenet of the Judeo-Christian worldview, narrowed the focus regarding who should have dominion over the creation.

A third idea, that of the "one true God," further defined the specialness of the chosen people. There may be other cultures and religions in the world, with other beliefs and different names for the creator, but there is only one true faith, and it is ours. Good Christians were called to proselytize the planet and convince others of their special truth: "Therefore, go and make disciples of all nations, baptizing them in the name of Father and of the Son and of the Holy Spirit, and teaching them to obey everything I have commanded you" (Matthew 28: 19–20). Christianity further restricted the parameters of truth and choseness by establishing their Messiah as the single arbiter at the gates of heaven. No one entered paradise except through him. The Catholic hierarchy later added the notion of the infallibility of the pope, which gave god-like qualities to the temporal laws and leaders of the church. The doctrine of the divine right of kings then extended infallibility and limitless power to selected political leaders. And since the church hierarchy was so vociferously patriarchal, at least half of humankind, namely women, were preemptively eliminated from the inner circle of authority and power.

These deeply held religious beliefs regarding dominion, choseness, the singularity of truth, the infallibility of church and temporal leaders, and the power of the patriarchy have provided the backdrop for the drama of White dominance. In many settings throughout the past 500 years these ideas have been manipulated politically to fuel the engine of Western expansion. The quest for land, wealth, and adventure were central drives, to be sure, but the cosmology of dominion and choseness has provided the religious and moral rationale, the sense of rightness that was necessary to justify the entire enterprise. In light of this, the single-dimensional sense of religious rightness that motivated the Islamist hijackers on September 11, 2001, is not dissimilar from that which has driven Christian acts of dominance and pre-emptive violence over the past two millennia.

Butler (1990) details this convergence of Christianity and dominance in his insightful analysis of the church's role in justifying slavery in the United States. He claims that it was the Christian concept of paternalistic authority that gave plantation owners their peculiar notions of control over the lives of enslaved Africans. Anglican concepts of authority "shaped a paternalistic ethic among planters," an ethic that

> not only coalesced with the doctrine of absolute obedience but made it all the more palatable and attractive. . . . Clergymen helped planters explain slave "misbehavior" in ways that solidified the masters' prejudices about slave degradation, and transformed planter views about laziness, lust, and lying among slaves into powerfully detailed pictures of African depravity. (p. 153)

Christianity and White dominance were similarly linked in Australia, as is demonstrated by the hubristic exuberance of John McDougall Stuart upon planting the Union Jack on a hill in the central desert:

> We then gave three hearty cheers for the flag, the emblem of civil and re-
> ligious liberty, and may it be a sign to the natives that the dawn of liberty,
> civilization, and Christianity is about to break upon them. (cited in Peach,
> 1984, p. 120)

Christian notions of dominion, choseness, singularity of truth, and divine
sanction of temporal patriarchal authority were well suited to the task of
justifying the institution of slavery, land theft, and other forms of White
supremacy.

These Christian notions are strikingly different from the cosmology of
most of the Indigenous people who became the targets of the Western drive
for dominion. Never in my conversations with Indigenous spiritual teachers throughout the world have I encountered the missionary zeal that has so
characterized the Christian tradition. Seldom have any of these Indigenous
groups sought to impose their spiritual cosmology on other people. Quite to
the contrary, their great struggle in the face of dominance has been to simply
preserve the integrity of their traditions in their own cultural communities.

In contrast to Western cosmologies, most Indigenous spiritual traditions also embody more respectful attitudes toward women and nature
(Cajete, 1993). Among the Ojibway of North America, for example, creation stories depict the earth as Mother and human beings as her children
(Johnston, 1995). Rather than having dominion over the earth, humankind
is dependent on her for our very survival. In Ojibway tradition the proper
role for human beings is to honor the earth as we would our mother, to
treat the earth with respect, as an altar upon which we carry out our lives.
The belief in earth-as-mother also grants intrinsic and high regard to the
role of women, which is vastly different from the commonly held biblical
image of Eve as an afterthought of creation, a mere helpmate for man, and
the prime cause for humankind's expulsion from paradise (Allen, 1992).

My purpose here is neither to demonize the Judeo-Christian worldview
nor to deify the universal goodness of Indigenous perspectives. I merely
seek to point out that some of the foundational principles of Western theology have been exploited in the service of dominance. Certainly, the Native
Peoples of the Americas and other parts of the world have had their own
internal issues of dominance and conflict across territorial and cultural
boundaries. Witness, for example, the Aztecs' relentless persecution of
neighboring groups or the Maoris' powerful warrior tradition that drove
out the original inhabitants of New Zealand. In sheer magnitude of dominance, however, none of these intergroup struggles between Indigenous
populations compares to the extent of Christianity's reach throughout the
world. By the end of the nineteenth century, the British alone had brought
one-fourth of the globe and one-fifth of the human race into the Christian

fold (MacLeod, 1997). Add to this the colonial grip established by France, Spain, Holland, and Portugal, and much of the planet's population was eventually subjected to the cosmology of Christendom.

It is important to point out that the Christian spiritual tradition itself has not been at fault in the establishment of White dominance, but rather the methods by which people in power have used Christianity to establish and defend White hegemony. Throughout history, the role of Christianity as related to issues of dominance and social justice has been mixed and complex. From liberation theology in Latin America, to civil rights leadership in the United States, to anti-apartheid resistance in South Africa, the Christian church in many ways has been a strong advocate for equity and social healing. The missionary movement may have been used as a tool in establishing Western colonial dominance, but the Christian vision has also inspired many people who have fought to unravel the destructive influences of that same missionary zeal. I trace my own passion for multicultural education to the vision of human dignity I learned through my early experiences in the church. In addition, Christianity today provides a spiritual base and a source of healing and inspiration for many people of color and Indigenous groups who are working for social change around the world.

But if our goal is to eliminate the deleterious effects of White dominance, then we must dig deeply into its causes. In order to free ourselves from the shackles of dominance, it is essential that we look at the shadow-side of Christian politics, including the predilection for single-dimensional truth and the proclivity for imposing spiritual hegemony over people of many different cultures. It is important to acknowledge that the assumption of rightness, which has sustained White racism and dominance for centuries, has also infected the roots of the very religious tradition that has inspired many of us who now seek to end dominance. In the spirit of Kingsolver's (1995) words at the opening of Chapter 2, we must seize the viper of rightness by the throat, look it straight in the eye, and own up to its venomous influence, even in our most cherished religious traditions.

The Luxury of Ignorance

The assumption of rightness is often reinforced by the fact that dominant groups tend to know very little about those people whom they define as "the other." Individuals from the dominant group are usually unaware of their own power and can carry on the daily activities of their lives without any substantial knowledge about, or meaningful interaction with, those people who are not part of the dominant group (Griffin, 1995; Howard, 1993; Johnson, 2001). This luxury of nonengagement, or "our sleep of unknowing" (O'Donohue, 2004, p. 49), is not available to members of marginalized

groups, whose "lives demand expertise in translation and transition" between their own culture and the culture of dominance (Griffin, 1995, p. 7).

In Australia, for example, most White Australians have very little
personal contact with Aboriginal people. Aboriginal people, on the other
hand, for their very survival, have had to cultivate a deep understanding
of White Australians. Since the early days of British invasion, Aboriginal
people have been studious observers of the moods, quirks, rituals, and
emotions of the White colonial psyche. They have had to know where they
are safe and where they are not, and how to devise strategies for survival
amidst the conditions of foreign occupation. Aboriginal young people today, like their African American counterparts in the United States, have to
be carefully taught by their elders how to read the intentions and avoid the
hostilities of Whites, particularly officials such as the police. By comparison, most White Australians know very little about the actual experiences
and feelings of Aboriginal people.

The luxury of ignorance was graphically demonstrated when I recently
attended a school board meeting in a community near Seattle, where a large
crowd of parents had gathered to argue the merits of expanding the district's foreign-language offerings. The proposal would have required the ex-
penditure of funds for additional teachers, an issue that was hotly contested
at the meeting. At one point, a frustrated father stood up and blurted out to
the assembled audience, "If English was good enough for Jesus Christ, it's
good enough for my kids!" As ridiculous as this comment may be, it under-
scores the simple-minded ease with which members of the dominant group
can structure a reality that supports their own limited assumptions.

Because of our dominant position, White perceptions and assumptions are often projected as truth into the larger world. Personal reality is
assumed to be actual reality. "Jesus is one of 'us'; therefore he must have
spoken English." "This is 'our' school; therefore 'they' don't belong here."
The process of projection is the foundation of the luxury of ignorance.
Although all human beings project their assumptions into the larger world,
Whites have the particular advantage of hegemonic social position to reinforce their limited images of truth (Tatum, 2002). Such familiar projections
and stereotypes as "Blacks are lazy" or "Indians are on welfare" have been
extremely resistant to change, precisely because they have been so deeply
inculcated into dominant-group perceptions of reality. Mistaking personal
and group judgments for actual descriptions of reality has been referred to
in social science literature as the "phenomenal absolutism error," a process
that is intrinsic to the luxury of ignorance and the perpetuation of dominance (Campbell, 1967, cited in Rothbart & John, 1993, p. 40).

Appleby (1992) likens the luxury of ignorance to "a deep forgetting"
that has clouded White awareness of the realities of history (p. 425). She

writes, "Most of what really happened in the colonial past was ignored because it fit so ill with the narrative of exceptionality" (p. 425). In the United States, and to a large extent in most of the lands invaded by Europeans, Whites were so fascinated with the "specialness" and the progress of their own colonial enterprise that they were either blind or irresponsive to the pain and destruction that resulted from their peculiar exceptionality. This was the real colorblindness: Whites seeing only in white. Thus, Griffin (1995) describes the United States as "a nation troubled by the bad dreams that come from repression and willed forgetting" (p. 10). This selective perception of reality is a function of our refusal to acknowledge those truths that collide with the legitimizing myths of White American specialness. The luxury of selective forgetting is not afforded those who have suffered the consequences of White dominance. For them, the American Dream has often become an unbearable nightmare.

Through the luxury of ignorance, Whites have for centuries maintained a view of reality that "makes sense" to us. Believing in our own legitimizing myths, we have been able to sustain a perception of our goodness, even in the face of the horrific destruction imposed on other people. Whites have had the power and the privilege, as we will see in the next section, to write our own versions of history. We have been able to determine the structure and content of schooling and in this way have institutionalized our ignorance in the name of education. Through the filter of our particular truth, we have projected only a narrow wavelength of light, usually tinted to favor our own countenance.

The Legacy of Privilege

Many privileges flow to Whites based solely on the color of our skin (McIntosh, 1988, 1989; Rodriguez & Villaverde, 2000; Wise, 2003). Simply feeling comfortable moving into a new neighborhood, or simply not having to wonder whether your colleagues perceive your new position as an affirmative action hire, are privileges that are usually invisible to White people. And in addition to being invisible, most of our privileges are also unearned. Sleeter (1996) states:

> As a White doctor's kid, who was doing well in school, teachers believed the best about me and treated me accordingly. Doors never closed to me, an experience I assumed to be universal. (p. 19)

Another privilege that comes unearned and invisible to Whites is the right to be seen as "the real Americans." All White people in America are foreign-born, or the descendents of foreign-born relatives, yet, because of the notion of Anglo-conformity discussed earlier, we are usually seen as the "standard" American (Bourne, 1916). The only "real" Americans, of course, are people of the Indigenous Nations, but they are usually left out of the equation and were not even offered citizenship in the United States until 1924. Related to this issue, my American Indian colleagues like to tease non–Indigenous Americans with the comment, "If only our tribes had established better immigration policies in the fifteenth century, we might have saved ourselves a lot of trouble."

From another perspective, Asian Americans are continually subjected to the "forever foreign" syndrome. Even well-educated White professionals will approach my colleague, David Koyama, and ask, "Where are you from?" His answer is always, "I'm from Seattle." They will persist, "Where are you really from?" He says, "I'm from the Wallingford neighborhood in Seattle." This isn't the direction in which the questioner wants to be going. In spite of the fact that David's Japanese American family has been in the United States for four generations, many people want to place them, and others who look like them, somewhere across the water. The security of not being questioned about one's personal identity, or not having to be seen as "fresh off the boat," is an additional privilege of Whiteness that often goes unacknowledged.

Studies of racial identification and self-perception in children, carried out in the 1940s and replicated in the 1990s, point to another area of privilege for Whites (K. B. Clark & Clark, 1947; Hinkle & Brown, 1990). In these studies Black children frequently made preferential choices for White dolls over Black dolls. Similarly, in my wife's inner-city classroom in the 1960s, Black children in the first grade were initially much less likely than White children to describe themselves in positive terms when looking in the mirror (Lotus Linton, personal communication, April 1969). The possibility of feeling good about oneself is a privilege that often comes invisibly to Whites as a mere function of our historical position of racial dominance.

Many of the privileges that continue to flow to Whites today are outgrowths of the colonial experience. American and British expatriates living in India, for example, continue to receive the rewards of a centuries-old system that has perpetuated the "making of masters in the servant's land" (Kidder, 1997, p. 158). Whites who would have an average middle-class lifestyle in the United States or England are able to live like royalty in India and other Third World nations. Simply by virtue of being White and Western, expatriates throughout the world enjoy the benefits of these "colonial remnants." And even those Whites who stay at home in their First World nations are supported daily by the continuing exploitation of lands and people in the colonialized world. The simple privilege of buying cheap french fries in a fast-food restaurant, for example, is supported by a complex system of dominance and subordination, wherein American-owned foreign agribusiness is destroying the culture, land base, and livelihood of peasant farm families 8,000 miles from my neighborhood burger stand (Apple, 1997). And in perhaps the most insidious exercise of privilege, people in power often manage to benefit financially from the tragedies of colonialized people, as demonstrated by this testimony from a Sri Lankan relief worker who saw Western corporations capitalizing on the reconstruction efforts in the wake of the 2004 tsunami: "The funds received for the benefit of the victims are directed to the benefit of the privileged few, not to the real victims. Our voices are not heard and not allowed to be voiced" (Klein, 2005, p.9).

Perhaps the most grievous characteristic of privilege is the social and psychological insulation that comes with dominance. The United States now has the richest adults and the poorest children of any Western nation (Males, 1996). This discrepancy is a function of both race and economics, since children of color are disproportionately represented in the ranks of poverty. Sadly, overwhelming numbers of well-to-do White folks support political efforts to provide tax breaks to the rich, which only serve to drive the nation into deeper deficits, thereby sacrificing any reasonable efforts to improve the present health and future prospects of poor children. Why do we allow the suffering of children in poverty to continue and even worsen in our country? Is it because the White people of our nation are uncaring and cruel? Whereas this may be true for some, a more plausible explanation is that so many of us are simply not touched by poverty. Privilege allows us not to know, not to see, and not to act. Privilege provides moral insulation against the cold winds of reality and awareness.

Finally, there is the privilege of "voice." Dominant groups have the power to control public discourse. Whites in Western nations have written the official history, established the systems of education, owned the media, directed the flow of funding, disproportionately influenced the political climate, and occupied the seats of power in most social institutions. Because of our social position, we have had the power to silence or interpret other people's voices and cultures. For example, groups attending the series of World Indigenous People's Conferences continually speak out against the "commodification of culture," which is the process whereby White anthropologists, explorers, missionaries, writers, scientists, and entrepreneurs have for centuries appropriated Indigenous culture for their own purposes and profit.

People from many different Indigenous groups have told me how their stories, arts, artifacts, spiritual objects, and even the bones of their ancestors have been collected and displayed in Western universities, laboratories, art galleries, books, theaters, museums, and shops (Bob Morgan, personal communication, June 2003). Through the series of World Conferences and other international forums, Indigenous people are now fighting for the legal recognition and protection of their property rights regarding the material and spiritual content of their cultural traditions.

Intentionally or unintentionally, we in the West have often been the consumers of other people's cultures, claiming their property as ours and projecting their images through the filter of our interpretation. This predilection for voicing other people's stories is not well received by our colleagues from other cultures. In the words of the preeminent African American playwright, August Wilson:

> We reject, without reservation, any attempt by anyone to re-write our history so as to deny us the rewards of our spiritual labors, and to become the cultural custodians of our art. (Quoted in Holmstrom, 1997, p. 15)

Even in our postmodern rhetoric related to the deconstruction of dominance, Whites often speak of "giving voice" to marginalized groups, as if *their* voice is *ours* to give. From our position of privilege, we have often attempted to construct the stage on which other people's dramas are enacted. We have even tried at times to play their parts. And, of course, we have usually sold the tickets.

Many privileges have come to Whites simply because we are members of the dominant group: the privilege of having our voices heard, of not having to explain or defend our legitimate citizenship or identity, of seeing our images projected in a positive light, of remaining insulated from other people's realities, of being represented in positions of power, and of being able to tell our own stories. These privileges are usually not earned and often not consciously acknowledged. That our privileged dominance often threatens the physical and cultural well-being of other groups is a reality that Whites, for the most part, have chosen to ignore. The fact that we *can* choose to ignore such realities is perhaps our most insidious privilege.

POSSIBILITIES FOR HOPE AND HEALING

White teachers often speak to me about their feelings of powerlessness regarding the tremendous odds working against us in the classroom. In the face of the pernicious and long-term effects of dominance, many of us become frustrated in our efforts to significantly alter the lives of our students, particularly those who have been most marginalized by dominance. Given the challenges confronting us, some well-intended and once idealistic teachers have fallen into despondency and even cynicism. Some, who once believed that all students could achieve, have lost faith in the face of the real difficulties in their students' lives and have come to blame the culture and characteristics of the child for the school's failure to effectively serve all of our students. Even Whites who have held true to our calling as educators continue to struggle with the issues of dominance, and we often ask ourselves: What can I do as a White teacher?

Much of our frustration as educators flows from the fact that the dynamics of dominance are self-perpetuating. The luxury of ignorance, the assumption of rightness, and the legacy of privilege have for centuries functioned together to support and legitimize White dominance. The interaction of these three dynamics has formed the "dominance paradigm," a pervasive and persistent worldview wherein White assumptions are held to be true and right, White ignorance of other groups is the norm, and White privilege flourishes essentially unchallenged and unacknowledged. The dominance paradigm has allowed Whites to continue to benefit from past and present dominance, with or without our conscious intent and awareness. It has created a "cultural encasement of meanings, a prison house of language and ideas" that has proven highly resistant to change (McLaren, 1988, p. 173).

By elucidating in this chapter the deeper issues of dominance, I have worried that White educators might feel either overwhelmed by the enormity of the challenge or perhaps blamed for the pains of the past. My intent has simply been to create a clearer understanding of the dynamics of dominance. My hope is that, by understanding the true nature of these dynamics, we can become highly competent diagnosticians of dominance, a skill that is essential to our role as transformationist White teachers in a multicultural nation.

For the remainder of the book I will argue that change is possible and that White educators do, indeed, have a significant and unique role to play in the healing process. Of course, we alone cannot solve all the problems left in the wake of dominance, but together with our students and colleagues of color there are many healing responses we can bring to the educational process. As White educators we represent only one of many influences determining the direction of schooling, but our collective presence has had disproportionate historical influence over the course of educational institutions. By redirecting the resources and the power that have been available to us because of dominance, we can be instrumental in shifting the flow of education toward greater equity and inclusion. Our responsibility as White educators is to understand the past and present dynamics of dominance in order that we might more effectively contribute to the creation of a better future for all of our students. How we might engage this personal and professional journey is the focus of the following five chapters.

CHAPTER 4

White Educators
and the River of Change

I've known rivers:
I've known rivers ancient as the world and older than the flow of
human blood in human veins.
My soul has grown deep like the rivers.
                    —Langston Hughes, "The Negro Speaks of Rivers"

At the age of twenty, my son lost his best friend, Matt, to a tragic death
in the gorge of the Rio Grande River. The two of them were like brothers,
having grown up together since second grade. None of us know for certain
what happened, except that Matt's body was found five miles downriver
from the Rio Grande bridge west of Taos, New Mexico. My son, Benjie,
was in his second year of college at the time. He came home at the end of
the fall term, two months after his friend died, and told his mother and
me that he was leaving school. He wanted to go to Taos and come to terms
with Matt's death. We were tempted at first to try to talk him out of it,
afraid that he might fall victim to his own depression and pain. But in the
end, we knew he had to go. He needed to mourn in his own way, by hiking
and skiing the Sangre De Cristo Mountains and kayaking the rapids of the
Rio Grande, which had taken his friend on his last journey.

Benjie's move to Taos was a mythic act of courage. He had chosen to
go into the den of the beast, to face directly the fear and the pain and the
confusion he felt. In Taos he met the young man who had been living with
Matt at the time of his death, and together they formed a strong bond that
helped to heal their mutual wound. In the gorge of the Rio Grande they
built a monument of remembrance to their friend and helped each other
through a long, cold New Mexico winter.

The next spring Benjie got a job with a white-water expedition company in the Grand Canyon of the Colorado River. He paid his dues there
as a flunky in the staging warehouse for three years and eventually ful-
filled his dream of becoming a certified river guide in what he calls "the
deepest ditch in the world." He now takes his customers on eight-day

adventures through the wildest water in the West and has fallen in love with the beauty and mystery of his new canyon home. What began for him as a journey of pain and loss in the Southwest has gradually transformed his life into a time of healing and discovery. He was wiser than I at the time he chose to go to Taos, and I am thankful now that I did not give in to my fears and temptations to interrupt his deeper instincts for growth. One of the greatest gifts of parenthood is that our children offer us so many opportunities to learn from their innate wisdom. In this sense, I identified deeply with Bill Cosby's comment after the tragic loss of his own son: "He was my hero."

THE RIVER OF DIVERSITY

Drawn into Benjie's adventures in the Grand Canyon, we now conduct an 8-day Colorado River workshop for educators each summer, and in this way my colleagues in the field are able to learn and grow from his experiences there. His story of tragic loss and gradual healing on the river has become a metaphor for my work in multicultural education. Using images and stories from the river, I also share the lessons I have learned from him with the thousands of educators I meet in schools and universities throughout the United States and Australia each year.

On my first journey into the Canyon, I learned that the Colorado is not merely one river. Along the 276-mile stretch between Glen Canyon Dam and Lake Mead, many streams and tributaries join the Colorado. Each stream flows down a unique and separate side canyon, bringing water and silt from miles away, far beyond the rim of the Canyon. The color of the river changes constantly as fresh deposits enter the main channel. And the colors of the many tributaries themselves are in continuous flux, depending on the level and distribution of rainfall in their particular drainage systems.

On a recent journey down the Colorado, the river was flowing clear and blue when we put in at Lee's Ferry. Soon, the Paria River brought a silt of whitish clay into the main channel, and the water took on a cloudy appearance. Later, the Little Colorado was flowing at high volume and added its thick and reddish-brown water to the Colorado, leaving it a rich and creamy ochre-brown. At the Havasu River we encountered a water of crystal-clear turquoise, the namesake of the Havasupai Indians who live in a small village in the side canyon, "the People of the blue-green water." Throughout the eight days of our journey, as we passed each new side canyon and observed each subtle shift in the texture and hue of the river, I thought of our rich racial, ethnic, and cultural diversity as a nation.

At its original source, the river of America was formed by the Native People of the continent. With their many languages, cultures, and traditional land bases, they were, and are still today, a richly varied stream. Then came the people of Europe, from different lands and cultures, and changed the river of America considerably upon their arrival. To this mixture came the people of Africa, who came locked in chains in the cargo bays of slave ships, not as willing immigrants. In spite of the pain and tragedy surrounding their arrival, Americans of African descent have added their rich and ancient cultural traditions to the river of America. Hispanic people were present as well, many of them mestizo, a mixture of Indian and European blood, a new people formed by the confluence of different streams that have contributed to the larger river. And the people of Asia came from their many cultures and homelands, adding even more currents of uniqueness to the larger river.

The river of America, like the Colorado, never stops changing. New streams are continually forming, bringing diverse religions, languages, cultures, tastes, styles, and traditions into the composite channel. As a nation, we are constantly influenced by both internal and external currents of change. Cultural groups within our borders evolve, adapt, migrate, intermarry with other groups, and transform themselves over generations and decades of change and flow. External events in Southeast Asia, Central America, Eastern Europe, the Middle East, and Africa stimulate the flow of more people and cultures into the larger river. As is true for the side canyons of the Colorado, those of us already on the river below cannot see all the historical and cultural terrain these new arrivals have traversed in their journey to join us in the river of America. We cannot know all that they have experienced in their homelands, yet they touch our lives, change us, and make us deeper and richer as a nation because of what they bring to our shared river.

I realize that this vision of the river of diversity may appear considerably idealized. In actual experience there has been much pain and struggle in these waters, particularly in those places where various cultural streams have met, in both the United States and other nations of the West. I have learned from my son that the wildest rapids along the Colorado are created in the confluences, those places where tributaries join the main river. Over eons of time, large floods in the side canyons have occasionally washed huge boulders into the main channel, sometimes completely stopping its flow. The river would build up tremendous pressure behind these temporary dams, and when it finally broke through, a major rapid would be left as a memory of the tumultuous event. These places of turmoil are the most exciting for white-water rafters, but they are also the most dangerous. The same is true for the confluence of cultures. The places where we meet across our differences as human beings can provide stimulating and adventurous opportunities for new learning, but they have also been places of pain, conflict, and loss, as was demonstrated in the discussion of White dominance in Chapter 2. The river of diversity offers both dangers and delights to those of us who choose to ply its ever-changing waters.

River guides say that the most dangerous places along the Colorado are the "hydraulics." These are deep holes of powerful recirculating current created on the downriver side of large boulders in the main channel. River guides know that the larger hydraulics can endanger even their 40-foot power rafts, holding them captive in the middle of the current or capsizing their passengers at the whim of the river. A guide must be familiar with the nature and location of these holes and respect their power. On the river of diversity, the holes are a metaphor for the dynamics of White dominance, which have been recirculating for centuries in our institutional practices and cultural assumptions and have always endangered our journey toward unity and social justice.

WHITE TEACHERS AND THE HEALING RESPONSE

Teaching in a multicultural society is like my son's story of becoming a river guide in the Grand Canyon. Benjie's tragic loss of his friend, his deep suffering, his courageous engagement with the source of his pain, and his eventual initiation into the process of healing on the river have a great deal to teach us about our role as educators in diverse settings. His experience has guided my approach to this book: to encourage White educators to look deeply into the nature of dominance, to understand as authentically as we can the reality of its tragic impact in the lives of our colleagues and students, and then to struggle and work together to create healing responses on the river of change.

Like my son's work on the Colorado, teaching confronts us with an enormous responsibility to help young people learn to navigate the often treacherous waters of racial identity development and intergroup relations. Regarding issues of dominance and cultural diversity, we need to know the nature and location of the many obstacles on the river, and we must have the awareness, knowledge, and skills to help our students enter the journey of life adequately prepared for both the dangers and the thrills of the ride. As was true for my son, our work on the river is often a function of healing, helping both ourselves and our students overcome the injustices imposed by past and present arrangements of dominance. Although this healing function is seldom written into our job descriptions, we know it is a necessary part of being with young people on the river of growth and change.

When discussing with teachers the many struggles and opportunities presented to us on the river of diversity, there is one question which inevitably surfaces: "What can I do as a White teacher?" Because of the complexity and pain associated with issues of dominance and diversity, it is understandable that White teachers would often feel inadequate and confused regarding their role in multicultural schools. In my work with teachers over the past 40 years, however, I have found that there are many significant contributions we can make to the healing process. In this section I will discuss four of these: honesty, empathy, advocacy, and action.

Honesty

As we saw in Chapter 3, the assumption of rightness and the luxury of ignorance are two dynamics that have been essential to the perpetuation of the dominance paradigm. Honesty challenges both of these. Honesty begins for Whites when we learn to question our own assumptions and acknowledge the limitations of our culturally conditioned perceptions of truth. This process began for me in my New Haven years, as recounted in Chapter 1. Until I was 18 years old, I had never experienced personal contact with anyone who was not White. I had not yet dipped a toe in the river of diversity. Even though my world was so narrowly circumscribed, I was seen by my teachers and peers as being a smart kid. I was a top student with high SAT scores, excellent recommendations, and a scholarship to a prestigious university. In spite of my academic accomplishments, however, I was utterly unprepared to understand the realities of the urban revolution taking place outside the Ivy walls of Yale in the late 1960s. I was highly competent in the White world, yet totally ignorant in the other. I was both smart and dumb at the same time. This simultaneous sense of intelligence and ignorance is an appropriate and healthy realization for White educators today, reminding us that intellectual achievement as measured from the perspective of Western institutions does not necessarily confer wisdom in the multicultural dimension (Jackman, 1981). Only by acknowledging our ignorance and honestly questioning our assumptions can we begin to unravel key elements of the dominance paradigm.

Several White educators and researchers have provided effective role models for an honest interrogation of Whiteness (Giroux, 1997b; Keeley, 1996; Kivel, 2002; McIntosh, 1988; Novick, 1995; Paley, 2000; Sleeter, 1999; Weiss et al., 1997; Wise, 2003). As White educators we have often been concerned with analyzing the effects of dominance on other groups, but seldom have we looked at dominance from the inside. As Kivel (1996) points out, "We never talk about what it means to be 'in here' with other White people" (p. 1). Similarly, McIntosh (1988) writes:

> In my place and class, I did not see myself as a racist because I was taught to recognize racism only in individual acts of meanness by members of my group, never as an invisible system conferring unsought racial dominance on my group from birth. (p. 81)

In her analysis of White privilege, McIntosh has exposed the invisible benefits of racism and enabled us to see ourselves in a new light. Similarly, Sleeter (1996) shares her honest appraisal of the insecurities and assumptions that many White educators carry into our work with students of color:

> Much as I cared for these kids, I had no notion of preparing them for college, had accepted low academic expectations of them, and had almost no academic content knowledge about anyone other than Euro-Americans. (p. 24)

Paley (1979, 2000) also speaks for many White teachers when she describes her discomfort in dealing directly with issues of race in the classroom. In her earlier years of teaching she would often brush aside or ignore negative racial comments by her students. She initially rationalized this behavior as a function of "politeness" but later acknowledged that her avoidance of these issues was actually masking a deep fear of her own feelings about race.

When White educators acknowledge both our insecurity and our privilege when dealing with issues of race, and when we begin to question the influence of the dominance paradigm in our work with students, we actually gain credibility with our colleagues and students from other racial and ethnic groups. It is refreshing for racial and cultural "others" to see that the critical lens of self-awareness can focus on the realities of Whiteness, rather than the deficiencies of "otherness." Writes bell hooks (1990):

> One change in direction that would be real cool would be the production of a discourse on race that interrogates whiteness. It would be just so interesting for all those white folks who are giving blacks their take on blackness to let them know what's up with whiteness. . . . Only a persistent, rigorous, and informed critique of whiteness could really determine what forces of denial, fear, and competition are responsible for creating fundamental gaps between professed political commitment to eradicating racism and the participation in the construction of a discourse on race that perpetuates racial domination. (p. 54)

Blacks and other historically marginalized groups have always been cognizant of White privilege, but when Whites ourselves finally come out of the closet of ignorance and denial we can begin to break down both the dominance paradigm and the barriers between us and other groups.

Whites can also contribute to the healing of dominance by demanding honesty in the teaching and construction of history. It is not the sole responsibility of historically marginalized groups to insist that their stories be accurately represented in the school curriculum. Honesty and fair representation ought to be a concern for all of us, and White parents and educators can lend considerable weight to the argument in favor of multicultural curriculum. This was clearly demonstrated for me when our eighth grade multicultural education program, Project REACH, came under attack in a predominantly White school district in the Puget Sound area of Washington State. A small group of parents, who were connected to one of the national Christian Right organizations, complained that our REACH materials threatened their family values and invaded their privacy. In part, their concerns had been inspired by Phyllis Schlafly's (1984) critique of REACH in her book *Child Abuse in the Classroom.* One aspect of our program that became a central focus for their complaint was the presentation of U.S. history from the multiple cultural perspectives of Native Americans, African Americans, Hispanic Americans, and Asian Americans. According to Schlafly's account, these REACH materials were "very derogatory toward the Caucasian" (p. 70).

The challenge to our multicultural curriculum culminated in a series of community hearings convened by the local school board, one member of which had recently been elected by running an anti-REACH campaign. Hundreds of parents, students, and community members attended these meetings, giving testimony for and against the REACH program. Fortunately for us, some 600 eighth grade students over a three-year period had participated in the program by the time of the hearings, and their voices along with those of their parents were overwhelmingly supportive of our multicultural approach. White students demanded the right to read history from different perspectives, and White parents insisted that their sons and daughters have this opportunity to prepare for life in a diverse society. American Indian students, along with their parents and leaders from the local reservation, were also active in these hearings, arguing that the schools should not abandon this one opportunity for a Native American historical perspective to be presented within the curriculum.

Based on strong testimony from students and community members, the board finally voted to retain the program and expand the multicultural focus to all grade levels. Even the board member who had been elected on the anti-REACH platform eventually voted in favor of the program. I was proud of the parents and students from all racial, ethnic, and cultural groups who spoke out in these hearings and defended not just the REACH program but also the deeper vision of quality education in a pluralistic nation. We discovered later that the small group of residents who brought the original challenge to the forefront were also involved in a prior dispute over tidal land rights with the local American Indian Nation. As it turned out, they did not want the Native American perspective to be shared in the district's history courses. Given the level of overt and subtle racism directed toward American Indians in this community, I doubt that we would have seen the same positive result from these hearings had there been no support from the White community. But by combining forces and becoming mutually co-responsible for voicing their common position, American Indian and White families together were able to convince even recalcitrant board members of the merits of an honest and multicultural portrayal of history.

As Abraham Lincoln said in his annual message to Congress in the difficult year of 1862, "We must disenthrall ourselves" because "the dogmas of the quiet past are inadequate to the stormy present" (cited in Levine, 1996, pp. xiv–xv). As Lincoln did for America in his day, so White educators can, for our time, help disenthrall our colleagues and communities of their loyalty to the old dogmas of dominance. In place of these limited constructs, we, along with our colleagues of color, can defend and promote more honest and continually updated versions of history, versions that acknowledge and explore the many authentic voices of our nation's people.

Empathy

In my son's many adventures in the Grand Canyon, he has had an opportunity to run the rapids in several different types of river craft, including small paddle boats, rowboats, dories, and kayaks, in addition to the large power rafts he normally operates. He tells me that each craft offers an entirely different experience of the river. Each has differing degrees of maneuverability and each takes the rapids in a unique way. The river itself actually looks and feels different from the vantage point of each craft. On the river of diversity, empathy provides a similar opportunity to view social reality from different perspectives. As a White American, I cannot fully experience the unique and complex realities of African Americans, American Indians, or Aboriginal Australians, nor can they actually experience what it is to be White. But we can occasionally share a part of the journey together, occupy the same craft for a time, and learn to see the river through each other's eyes.

In my travels to Australia I have developed a friendship with an Iranian Muslim faculty member at a university in Sydney. On the first day of one of our recent workshops, he reported to me that his 10-year-old daughter had been very excited that morning about a multicultural day at her school. She had decided to wear her traditional clothing and tell her classmates about her culture. But as my friend drove her up to the door of the school, she panicked. When she didn't see anyone else in traditional clothing, she sunk down in the car seat. She didn't want to go to school. Her father left her there because he had to go to work, but felt sad when he drove away. When he told me this story, we shared the moment of sadness together. I am neither Iranian nor Muslim, but as a father and a friend I could feel his pain and that of his daughter. I was angry at all the forces that would cause a little girl to cringe in shame simply because she wore to school a beautiful outfit that at home in her own culture would be proudly celebrated.

Empathy means "to feel with." Empathy requires the suspension of assumptions, the letting go of ego, and the release of the privilege of non-engagement. In this sense, empathy is the antithesis of dominance. It requires all of our senses and focuses our attention on the perspective and worldview of another person. I did not *become* Iranian or Muslim when I listened to my friend's story, but I could attune my empathetic capacity to his feelings as a father. I could not fully *know* what he was experiencing, but I could be *with* him in this moment.

Empathy is a healing response because it allows us as Whites to step outside of dominance, to see our social position in a new light, and connect with the experience of others who see the river of diversity from a different perspective. This happened for my daughter, Jessie, when she traveled to snowboard in Wyoming with her husband, Eric, who is African American. His dream upon graduating from college had been to snowboard for an entire winter in Wyoming. When Jessie joined him there, however, he was only two months into his adventure but already feeling discouraged. He felt uncomfortable living in a resort town where he had not yet been able to locate more than five other Black people. He worried about his safety when some of the locals would drive slowly by him on isolated mountain roads and stare coldly from the rifle-racked cabs of their pick-up trucks.

Jessie's empathetic concern for Eric removed some of the comfortable insulation that is usually provided by White privilege. Through his eyes she experienced this particular location in an entirely different way than she would with a White partner. It was also important to Eric that she could understand his concerns and could support him in his eventual decision to leave Wyoming. In reflecting on the lessons of his sadly shortened adventure, Eric told me recently, "I tried at first to explain to my

White friends why I came back early from Wyoming, but then I gave up. They didn't seem to get it. Nothing really blatant or obvious happened—it was just the constant feeling of not being comfortable, a subtle threat that was always there." It is important for us as White educators to realize that many of our students of color have these feelings much of the time in the classroom (Steele, 2004).

Empathy invites us to listen to other people's stories, to see the world of cultural differences in the authentic light of those who must deal with dominance on a daily basis. My colleague Colleen Almojuela has told me, "As an American Indian person I can never 100% isolate myself from dominance. If I go to the hills and try to get away, even then I am hiding from dominance. It still determines my life." Similarly, Sonia Nieto (1996) says of her own high school experience that "I had come to feel somewhat ashamed of speaking Spanish and wanted to make it very clear that I was intelligent in spite of it" (p. 2). Many young people of color, even successful students like Nieto and Almojuela, often experience considerable emotional tension in school because of persistent pressure around the "choice between belonging and succeeding" (Nieto, 1996, p. 3). Likewise, Cornell West (1993b) reminds us that many African American young people suffer from profound "existential angst" resulting from the "ontological wounds and emotional scars inflicted by White supremacist beliefs and images permeating U.S. society and culture" (p. 17). This perpetual tension is a major contributor to the race-based achievement gap, and is an issue we will revisit in more detail in our discussion of "stereotype threat" in Chapter 7 (Aronson, 2004; Aronson & Steele, 2005; Rosenthal, 2002; Steele, 2004).

In my own eighth-grade classroom several years ago, I had a Japanese American student who had experienced the wounds and scars of racial harassment throughout her career in our predominantly White school district. She always dealt with these situations by fighting, which caused her a great deal of trouble with school authorities, who usually didn't understand the constant anger she felt. We developed a good friendship over the year, and she wholeheartedly participated in the multicultural activities in our classroom. At our REACH Cultural Fair she presented a display of her family history, and she and her mother came dressed in their beautiful hand-sewn kimonos, sharing food and stories from their Japanese American culture. Many years later, when she was in her mid-twenties, I met her at a social event, where she said to me, "Gary, I never told you this, but the REACH program kept me in school. After I did my Cultural Fair project, some of the people who had been giving me the hardest time stopped bugging me. It seemed like there was more respect after that. I don't think I would have stayed in school if things hadn't gotten better."

As White educators, we cannot fully know or experience the struggles of our students and colleagues of color, but we can work to create an empathetic environment in which their stories and experiences can be acknowledged and shared. Too often, the legacy of privilege and the luxury of ignorance have prevented us from seeing and hearing one another. Even though we are attempting to work and learn together in the same schools, we have been separated by the culture of power that was established in the wake of dominance (Delpit, 2002; Sleeter, 2001). We may occupy the same physical space, but at the level of the heart we have been traveling in separate boats. White educators can contribute to the dissolution of these barriers when we suspend the assumptions of dominance and begin to view the schooling experience through the eyes of those who have been marginalized by it. Writes Delpit (1995):

> When we teach across the boundaries of race, class, and gender—indeed when we teach at all—we must recognize and overcome the power differential, the stereotypes and the other barriers which prevent us from seeing each other. (p. 134)

Empathy begins with seeing others in their own light rather than through our projections of them in our light. Delpit (1995) quotes two African American teachers who were frustrated with their seemingly futile efforts to communicate with their White colleagues: "They think they know what's best for everybody, for everybody's children" and "They don't really want to hear what you have to say. They wear blinders and ear plugs" (pp. 21–22). These comments echo the sentiments of the Native American parents in my local school district, who were upset with the disproportionate number of referrals of their children to special education (Chapter 2). We were able in that situation to overcome some of the barriers of cultural difference only when we enable White teachers to acquire a deep personal connection with the actual perspectives of Indian parents, educators, and students.

Our "Indian Child in the Classroom" inservice course, as described in Chapter 2, was an exercise in empathy. It proved to be an effective healing response because it reversed the power differential in our school district. Rather than diagnosing the "deficiencies" of Indian children from the perspective of the dominance paradigm, the course required us as White educators to challenge our assumptions and face the limitations of our own knowledge. We asked ourselves, "What am I not seeing here? How are my assumptions and behaviors getting in the way of serving American Indian children? Who can help me overcome the deficiencies in my own perceptions?" Empathy actually opened the door of personal and professional growth for White educators in our district, enhanced our effectiveness as teachers, and relieved us of the illusion that we alone have the right answers for other people's children.

Advocacy

Every organization has its own circle of power, an in-group of influence that is populated by those individuals who, through a combination of numbers, position, resources, and access to privileged information, are able to exert disproportionate control over the decision-making process. In my work in schools throughout the United States and Australia, I have found that people of color often feel excluded from these circles of power in educational organizations. White educators have had greater "authority to establish what was considered to be 'truth' regardless of the opinions of people of color" (Delpit, 1995, p. 26). As White educators committed to equity and social justice, we can offer a significant healing response when we advocate for the inclusion of historical "others" in the circle of power.

Henry Louis Gates, Jr. (1997) tells a story that illustrates the advocacy process. When he was being recruited by Harvard to become chair of the Department of Afro-American Studies, he made an unusual and strategic request. He had been negotiating for some time with Henry Rosovsky, dean of the Faculty of Arts and Sciences at Harvard, and they had reached agreement on all points. At the very end of the negotiations, however, Gates raised one final issue. Rosovsky was a brilliant administrator, and since Gates had no previous administrative experience, he asked Rosovsky to fly him to Boston for a series of Friday afternoon meetings to "tell me how to be a successful administrator." Gates wanted to know the nature of the circle of power at Harvard, to gain access to information that is not often shared with those outside that circle. Rosovsky agreed, and over a period of several months he passed on to Gates his knowledge of the politics of power at Harvard, and put him in contact with key people whose support would be crucial in the new position. With his own brilliance and depth of vision, Gates surely would have achieved success without the advocacy of a White professor and administrator, but the process may have proven more difficult, lengthy, and painful.

Besides opening the circle of power to those who have historically been marginalized by it, the work of advocacy also involves reeducating many of our White colleagues who are not ready for such inclusion. Those of our peers who have not ventured far in their own journeys down the river of diversity are often in particular need of new information and perspectives. Too often in the past, the burden of reeducating Whites has fallen on the shoulders of people of color. One of my Aboriginal colleagues, for example, a prominent educational leader in Australia, is frequently asked to speak to White audiences there. For many years he has given generously of his time, but he has recently become discouraged by the responses he receives. After sharing his personal and political perspectives on Aboriginal issues, he is invariably asked insulting and ignorant questions, such as, "Why do Aboriginal people tear apart the houses that the government builds for them?" "Why is there so much alcoholism among your people?" "Why are your people unwilling to work?"

Each of these questions raises complex issues, and considerable energy is required to educate White Australians about the realities of history and the continuing effects of dominance. My friend is growing weary of responding to such uninformed inquiries from his White audiences and wants to put more energy into helping his own people. Aboriginal people, like all marginalized groups, have enormous issues to deal with in their own communities and should not have to be continually responsible for reeducating Whites. White educators and leaders in the White community should take on the responsibility of undoing White ignorance, rather than relying on people from other racial groups to carry this burden. It is important for us to realize that we can make a significant contribution to the healing process when we reeducate our White students, colleagues, and family members regarding the realities of dominance.

One example of how we might contribute to the reeducative process for our White colleagues has to do with the ongoing debate over affirmative action. I find that many White educators, as well as leaders in business and community organizations, believe that policies of affirmative action have gone too far, that the playing field of opportunity has been leveled, and that it is perhaps even tilted now in favor of women and people of color. These sentiments were certainly evident in the victory of Proposition 209 in California, as well as in the passage of similar anti–affirmative action measures in other states. Such sentiments are also prevalent in the workplace, as was made clear in a comment recently addressed to me by a White senior executive in a large corporation: "I tell my college-aged son that the deck is now stacked against him and that he'll have to work twice as hard as Blacks or women because most of the opportunities are going to them."

Most attacks on affirmative action are based on the issue of fairness—for the sake of fairness we ought to end "special preferences for special groups." Responding to this line of argument, I frequently remind my White peers that the Founding Founders, by insuring that only White, male, property owners would, for the most part, be provided full participation in the polity of the new nation, effectively established America's first affirmative action policy. This preferential treatment for White males, which has been in place for well over two centuries, has been quite effective in guaranteeing that this protected class of individuals would remain in positions of power. Indeed, the vast majority of Fortune 500 corporate CEOs, university presidents, and school superintendents in the United States are White, male, property owners. The legacy privilege of affirmative action for White males continues to work well for them. In comparison, affirmative action for women and people of color has been in effect for just over four decades and is only gradually beginning to make headroads into the highest levels of power.

Given our two centuries of preferential treatment, I suggest to my White male colleagues that their arguments against affirmative action ought to be based on something other than "fairness." There are many valid reasons to regularly adjust and refine our ongoing affirmative action policies, but fairness in the form of parity is still a distant dream. If fairness, simply in terms of number of years of preferential treatment, were our goal, then affirmative action for women and people of color would be in place well into the twenty-second century! By thus presenting an alternative perspective on issues of race, in this case a perspective that challenges the knee-jerk reaction against affirmative action, we can stimulate a healthy measure of cognitive dissonance in the minds of our White colleagues. Such carefully targeted acts of advocacy can lead to those beneficial "train wrecks in the mind" that help facilitate the reeducative process for Whites. Through acts of advocacy we can begin to undermine some of the assumptions that have grown from centuries of dominance.

Action

The healing responses of honesty, empathy, and advocacy can become particularly powerful when combined with social action. Transformative action is the highest goal of multicultural education (J. A. Banks, 2004; Sleeter, 2001). Every act of teaching is a political act (Freire, 1970; Kriesberg, 1992; Parker, 2003). Once we become aware of the persistent and pernicious nature of dominance, we begin to realize that each choice we make regarding educational structure, process, content, curriculum, or pedagogy has implications for equity and social justice. For White educators who have become aware of dominance, the central question is, "Having described White privilege, what will I do to end it?" (McIntosh, 1989, p. 12). We are not responsible for having been born White, but we are accountable for how we respond to racism and dominance in our schools and communities today (Kivel, 1996; Kozol, 2005).

Acts of acknowledgment, in themselves, can serve a strong educative and transformative function. For example, when the bishops of ten leading Christian denominations in the Pacific Northwest issued a public apology to the Indigenous people of the Americas for the use of Christianity as a tool of conquest and oppression, a significant message was sent to all Christians and all Americans ("Bishops' Apology," 1987). Likewise, when the Southern Baptist Convention publicly confessed in 1995 to the "sin of racism" in the establishment of their denomination in the wake of the Civil War, this acknowledgment in itself was a source of enlightenment and healing for their membership and the nation as a whole (White, 1995). Similarly, when officials in the small Florida town of Sanford issued a formal apology for the racist actions of their townspeople in forcing Jackie Robinson off the local minor league baseball diamond in 1946, they educated everyone engaged in the 50th-year celebration of Robinson's major league debut (Wulf, 1997).

When the United States Senate in 2005 finally passed a resolution apologizing for its failure throughout the 19th and 20th centuries to enact legislation outlawing lynching (over 200 anti-lynching bills were introduced and all of them defeated), one of the sponsors of the bill, Senator Mary Landrieu of Louisiana, remarked, "This has been an extremely emotional, educational experience for me. This was domestic terrorism, and the Senate is uniquely culpable" (USA Today, June 16, 2005, p. 8). Although pronouncements such as these have in most cases been sadly and tragically delayed, such acts of public acknowledgment can bring the clear ring of truth to our national and global discussions of dominance and social justice. Our students, colleagues, and communities have a right to know both the pains and the glories of our common history. We as White educators can help open the door to healing by assuring that the full story of dominance is allowed to be expressed through the many aspects of our school curriculum, both formal and informal. Once suffering is acknowledged, it can be dealt with. If left repressed or denied, however, suffering only festers and pushes the pain ever deeper. Dominance, when left unacknowledged, merely perpetuates itself.

In light of this, the Canadian Royal Commission on Aboriginal Peoples completed in 1996 a 5-year inquiry into the historical struggles and contemporary challenges facing Canada's Native people. In their report the Commission extensively documented both the past and present effects of White dominance in the lives of Canada's Native people. Matthew Coon, grand chief of the Cree Nation in Quebec, said in response to the Commission's work, "The time has come for this country to confront its history. It's going to be a real social time bomb if grievances aren't addressed" (cited in Nickerson, 1996, p. 1). Coon's comment clearly reminds us that our efforts to acknowledge the effects of dominance must be followed by action to address the legacy of dominance. Without action for social justice, mere acknowledgment becomes a particularly cynical form of White privilege. Similar time bombs of pain and selective forgetting are presently ticking in many places throughout the world. As White educators committed to social justice, we can help assure that any explosions that might occur from these time bombs of selective forgetting will be those of enlightenment and positive change, rather than anger, denial, and continuing violence.

Besides acknowledging the pain of the past, we as White educators and citizens must also invest our attention, energy, and resources in the actual process of change. We can contribute to the demise of dominance by speaking out against racism when we see it reflected in the words and behaviors of our students, colleagues, neighbors, and families. Our individual acts of speaking out may not always have national and global repercussions, but they can be a powerful reeducative influence in the lives of the people we encounter each day.

When I was shopping for a new car, for example, I went to my local dealership and found exactly the Toyota I wanted. Having done my homework, I was able to negotiate an even better price than I thought was possible. When my wife and I sat down in the manager's office to sign the final papers, I was excited to close the deal and drive away in our new car. He knew I was getting a good deal, and just before handing me the sales agreement, he said, "You know, Gary, if you were a 'gook' I wouldn't give this low price." After hearing this, I went into a silent state of shock and lowered my head while he chattered on about the deal I was getting. I was angry. I didn't want to lose the car, but I couldn't accept the idea of giving this person my business. Finally, I raised my head from the papers and looked him in the eye and said, "Excuse me, but you've just ended the deal. I can't go through with this. The comment you just made is an insult to me and to my friends and colleagues who are Asian. Do you realize you are selling an Asian product? I hope this is the last time you use that term to describe another human being."

We walked out and have never returned to that dealership. I don't know if the manager learned anything from our encounter, but I hope that he might have. Often the lines of action are not drawn as decisively as they were in this instance, and there have been other times when I did not respond as clearly or effectively. It is easier to oppose dominance in theory than in practice, but it is a healing lesson for all of us to realize that we have the right and the power to interrupt the ongoing flow of racism when it confronts us in our daily lives. It can be particularly powerful when Whites choose to take this kind of action.

As White educators we can also do many things in our classrooms to support healing on the river of diversity. Much has been written about the theory and practice of multicultural education as a strategy for reinforcing democratic pluralism and social justice (C. A. M. Banks, 2005; J. A. Banks, 2004; Giroux, 1997a; Nieto, 1996; Sleeter, 1996). Chapter 7 will address in some detail the many ways that we as White educators can invite our students and colleagues into a deep and ongoing process of transformative inquiry and growth. From the broad perspective being considered here, the multicultural education process engages us in at least five key arenas of learning:

1. To know who we are racially and culturally
2. To learn about and value cultures different from our own
3. To view social reality through the lens of multiple perspectives
4. To understand the history and dynamics of dominance
5. To nurture in ourselves and our students a passion for justice and the skills for social action

When we structure our teaching and learning around these five basic components of multicultural education, we are contributing to the creation of a more just and open society. By participating in the process of equity pedagogy, we come to see that every act of teaching is a multicultural encounter in which the diverse realities of our students' lives can be both acknowledged and informed (C. A. M. Banks & Banks, 1995). When we foster a shared space of openness and trust within our schools and classrooms, we are dispelling the "cacophony of disparate voices claiming hegemony" that has too often in the past blocked our efforts to engage in honest dialogue on the river of diversity (Nieto, 1998, p. 23). When we allow the rich stories of diversity to be told and the deeper lessons of history to be learned in the classroom, we are opening both ourselves and our students to the possibility of change. And when we nurture in our students a vision of themselves as the agents of that change, we are reinforcing the essential foundation of pluralistic and participatory democracy.

FROM SOCIAL DOMINANCE TO SOCIAL JUSTICE

The dynamics of White dominance have been a pervasive and persistent force in the United States and other nations of the West. Throughout our history, the dominance paradigm has functioned as an obstacle to justice and equity on the river of diversity. In our exploration of the methodologies of dominance in Chapter 2, we saw that White hegemony was established by the conscious and willful intent of people in power. Subsequently, in our effort to decode the dominance paradigm in Chapter 3, we discovered that the assumption of rightness, the luxury of ignorance, and the legacy of privilege were so deeply imbedded in all of our major social institutions that White dominance eventually became self-perpetuating, continuing to manifest its pernicious presence with or without our awareness and intent.

In spite of the heavy weight of the past, however, it is my conviction that White dominance is neither inevitable nor invincible. Contrary to the rather pessimistic assumptions underlying social dominance theory (Sidanius & Pratto, 1993), I believe that systems of group-based inequality, which were originally established by choice and intent, can also be overcome through equally focused vision and will (C. S. Fischer et al., 1996). White educators can and must be instrumental in providing responses that heal. Through our efforts to establish honesty, create empathy, provide advocacy, and take action for change, we can join with our colleagues of color in a common initiative to decode and dismantle the dynamics of dominance. White educators who are willing to embark, both personally and professionally, on the river of diversity can begin to shift the flow of power away from oppression and toward greater inclusion and justice.

Just as the Colorado River became a source of healing and personal transformation for my son, so our work in education can open for us a journey of discovery, growth, and renewal. And just as my son had to pay his dues in the process of acquiring the knowledge and skills to become a river guide in the Grand Canyon, so White educators must do the necessary work to prepare ourselves for our role as effective agents of change in a multicultural nation and world. To this end, we must engage ourselves in both the inner and the outer work of personal and social transformation. At a minimum, this work entails the deep analysis of White dominance presented in Chapters 2 and 3, as well as a lifelong commitment to the process of our own racial identity development, which will be the focus of the following two chapters.

CHAPTER 5

Mapping the Journey of White Identity Development

When I was a child, I spoke like a child, I thought like a child, I reasoned like a child. When I became an adult, I gave up childish ways.   —I Corinthians 13:11

During my undergraduate years at Yale in the late 1960s, I became embroiled in the cross-currents of four simultaneous social movements: civil rights, anti-war, women's liberation, and campus reform. Being deeply engaged with each of these paradigmatic shifts, I experienced considerable realignment of my previously held sentiments and beliefs. For me this was a tumultuous time for identity development. I lived in an inner-city neighborhood through three summers of riots, worked with Black youths in several inner-city programs, entered my first committed relationship with a woman, lived with her in a student-created halfway house for mental patients transitioning back into "the real world," and started the first counterculture commune in New Haven. In addition, I experienced a crisis of conscience over the war in Vietnam and ultimately joined the movement to openly resist the draft. Through these years of personal dislocation and rapid social change, none of my patriotic beliefs or middle-class Christian values remained unexamined or unscathed. "Real" life seemed crazier than the delusions of my officially insane roommates in the halfway house, and I often felt adrift in a sea of vacuous identity.

It was in this context that I became fascinated with Erik Erikson's work on the stages of identity development in children and adults. The conceptual framework he presented in *Childhood and Society* (1950/1963) described the unfolding story of my own life. In the midst of the intensity and free-floating anxiety I felt at that time, Erikson's formulation provided a sense of comfort and stability. His stages of identity development anticipated many of my questions and embedded my struggle in a naturally unfolding process of growth and maturity. His theory named the stages of identity development and posed key questions for each transition in the life cycle.

It was helpful, for example, for me to realize that "identity versus identity confusion" was the central challenge facing me in the transition from adolescence to early adulthood. From the perspective of his work, it was natural that in my early twenties I should be challenging many of the assumptions and values I had acquired in my childhood. His analysis of early adulthood gave me confidence that my own emotions and experiences were legitimate and appropriate for that stage of my life. His work was growth-oriented rather than deficiency-oriented. It helped me see that my struggles were a natural part of the life-cycle transition into adulthood. Most important, his work gave meaning to my search for authentic identity by placing it in the context of a worthy and universal human drama.

Erikson's theory of identity development has greatly influenced my work with White teachers in multicultural education over the past four decades. Inspired by his approach, I have found it helpful to acknowledge that the development of a positive White racial identity, like the movement toward mature adulthood, is a continually unfolding journey of discovery and growth. Remembering the vulnerability and inadequacy I experienced in my own early adulthood, I know that many White educators are similarly subjected to insecurities and personal dislocations when confronted with issues of race. The affirmation I received from Erikson's nonjudgmental descriptive approach has served as a constant reminder for me to employ similar positive regard when working with my colleagues on issues of race and Whiteness.

There are many variations in the story of White identity development. In this and the following chapter I will explore some of the universal themes that emerge from this lifelong process of growth. I will attempt to identify the significant landmarks that can guide our journey toward an authentic and healing engagement with White identity. Precisely because our social reality is so highly racialized (Allen, 1999; Omi & Winant, 1993; Rodriguez & Villaverde, 2000), it is important for each of us to understand our own position and level of awareness vis-a-vis the categories of race. If we are to be effective navigators for ourselves and others on the river of diversity, it is important that we become self-reflective regarding our White identity. Wherever each of us may be in our own journey, it is liberating to realize that we can continue to grow and deepen in our understanding of what it means to be White educators in a multicultural society.

THEORIES OF RACIAL IDENTITY DEVELOPMENT

None of us are born with an integrated sense of racial identity. In my own case, I didn't become conscious of issues of race until I was 18 years old.

As we have seen from our discussion in previous chapters, race itself is a social construct, a learned category. Its meaning is communicated through interaction with our own and other racial groups. Many of us are inculcated with more negative images than positive regarding racial categories, necessitating considerable unlearning and reevaluation in the process of acquiring positive racial attitudes and identity.

Theories of racial identity development are well-established in the social science literature (Carter, 1995; Cross, 1971; Helms, 1990; Tatum, 1992, 2003). In these theories race is viewed as a socially and psychologically constructed process, not a fixed biological characteristic (Giroux, 1997b; Mukhopadhyay & Henze, 2003; Omi & Winant, 1986). From the perspective of racial identity development theory, each individual demonstrates differing degrees, styles, or stages of identification with his or her particular racial group. Helms (1990) defines racial identity as "a sense of group or collective identity based on one's perception that he or she shares a common racial heritage with a particular racial group" (p. 3). Theories of racial identity development are primarily concerned with the social, psychological, and political implications of our perceptions, beliefs, and behaviors regarding racial categories.

In terms of racial identity, it is important to point out that Whites, for the most part, are not accustomed to seeing ourselves as racial beings (Carter, 1995). As J. H. Katz and Ivey (1977) observe, "White people do not see themselves as being White" (p. 486). And as Helms (1990) notes, "if one is a White person in the United States, it is still possible to exist without ever having to acknowledge that reality" (p. 54). Even though the invisibility of Whiteness is gradually being eroded by the increasing racialization of public discourse and media images (Giroux, 1997b, 2000; Pence & Fields, 1999), it is still possible for Whites to exercise the privilege of choice regarding whether or not they will attend to their own identity as racial beings. The dynamics of dominance and the politics of difference, as we saw in Chapters 2 and 3, continue to allow Whites in Western nations to exist in the ironic and contradictory state of being blind to our own racial identity, on the one hand, while asserting the inherent superiority of Whiteness, on the other. Helms (1990) has suggested that Whites can overcome this history of ignorance and superiority by attending to several key developmental issues:

> The White person's developmental tasks with regard to development of a healthy White identity . . . require the abandonment of individual racism as well as the recognition of and active opposition to institutional and cultural racism. Concurrently, the person must become aware of her or his Whiteness, learn to accept Whiteness as an important part of herself or him-

self, and to internalize a realistically positive view of what it means to be White. (p. 55)

My purpose in this chapter and the next is to explore how we as White educators can grow beyond the limits of dominance, how we can come to terms with the realities of Whiteness, and how we can learn to transform both our own racial identity and the institutions that have perpetuated White hegemony.

Stages of Black Racial Identity Development

Because theories of White racial identity development have been based on earlier research related to the stages of Black identity, it is important to briefly review this prior work. Cross (1971, 1978, 1991) established a five-stage theory of Black identity development, including preencounter, encounter, immersion/emersion, internalization, and internalization-commitment. In the preencounter stage, African Americans tend to distance themselves from their own racial identity. There is an attempt to deny the importance of race, to contend that an individual can be judged on his or her own merits, irrespective of race. According to Tatum (1992), a Black person in this stage has "absorbed many of the beliefs that 'White is right' and 'Black is wrong'" (p. 331). Although we are focusing here on Black identity development, the process is similar for people from other marginalized groups. An American Indian colleague, for example, describes her preencounter stage as "wearing the mask of Whiteness" (Almojuela, Narratives[2]).

Transition to the next stage, encounter, is often stimulated by experiences or events that lift the mask of Whiteness and point out the significance of racial categories. An African American person, for example, may be subjected to personal villification and/or racist comments in spite of his or her best efforts to conform to dominant-culture norms and expectations. An African American colleague, who is dean of the graduate school at a large urban university, recounted such an experience at a recent workshop. He told of driving his new BMW through a White neighborhood and being stopped by a White police officer who confronted him with the question, "Where did you get this car?" My friend responded, "I bought it, and you can buy one, too, if you have enough money." To this the officer said, "Are you getting smart with me?" My colleague reflected

---

2. In preparing the text for this and the following chapter, I asked several White teachers and colleagues of color to write personal narratives regarding their own experiences with Whiteness. Several quotations from these narratives are included here and are referenced in the text to the "Narratives."

on this experience: "No matter how many academic degrees I may have, and no matter how prestigious my position in the university may be, in this confrontation with the police, I was just one more suspicious Black male driving a fancy car through a White neighborhood. This cop made his feelings clear that I didn't belong in either that car or that neighborhood." Similarly, Almojuela says of her transition to the encounter stage, "Negative experiences began to pound at me and caused my protective shell to chip away" (Narratives). In the encounter stage there is a realization that race alone, independent of other qualities of the individual, can lead to negative treatment.

Encounter experiences often lead to the next stage, immersion/emersion, which is characterized by anger toward Whites and avoidance of anything that rings of Whiteness. In this stage, according to Parham (1989), "Everything of value in life must be Black or related to Blackness. This stage is also characterized by a tendency to denigrate White people" (p. 190). An individual in the immersion/emersion stage is deeply committed to Blackness and invests much energy in exploring the roots of his or her Black culture, over and against that of Whites.

The next stage, internalization, begins when the "pro-black attitude becomes more expansive, open, and less defensive" (Cross, 1971, p. 24). Internalization is characterized by a greater willingness to interact with members of other groups, including Whites. A transition to the fifth stage, internalization-commitment, is evidenced by the individual's willingness to proactively engage in work that supports and strengthens the Black community. Individuals in this final stage are firmly and securely rooted in their own Black identity but also able to participate effectively in a broader multicultural context. West (1993b) writes:

> Mature Black identity results from an acknowledgement of the specific Black responses to White supremacist abuses and a moral assessment of these responses such that the humanity of Black people does not rest on deifying or demonizing others. (p. 28)

Stages of White Racial Identity Development

Building on previous research on Black identity, most of the early work exploring White racial identity formation was related to the issue of racism (Gaertner, 1976; Ganter, 1977; Jones, 1972; Kovel, 1970). These theorists assumed that White identity in Western nations was inherently tied to racism, and they attempted to describe the process whereby individual White people could learn to acknowledge and overcome their own racism. Later works by Hardiman (1979), Helms (1984, 1990, 1994, 1996), Carter (1995), and Leach, Behrens, and LaFleur (2002), explore the additional dimension of Whites' attempts to define a positive, as well as nonracist, sense of White cultural identity. These later works acknowledge that White identity must be defined not only in terms of racism but also in relation to an authentic sense of racial identity for White people. Consistent with this perspective, any comprehensive theory of White racial identity must explore the following three developmental tasks:

1. Acknowledging the reality of White racism in its individual, institutional, and cultural manifestations
2. Abandoning racism and engaging in active resistance to its many forms
3. Developing a positive, nonracist, and authentic connection to White racial and cultural identity

Because Helms's work is based on extensive empirical investigation that meets each of these three criteria, I have chosen to explore her approach in greater detail in this section.

Helms (1994, 1996) and Helms and Piper (1994) describe six stages in the development of White racial identity. The six stages are divided into two phases as follows:

PHASE I: ABANDONMENT OF A RACIST IDENTITY
Contact
Disintegration
Reintegration

PHASE II: ESTABLISHMENT OF A NONRACIST WHITE IDENTITY
Pseudo-Independence
Immersion-Emersion
Autonomy

In my review of each of the above stages, I will draw on previous descriptive summaries provided by Helms (1990), Tatum (1992), and Carter (1995).

Contact. Through encounter with the "other," White people are initiated into the process of racial identity development. Contact may occur personally, through meeting a friend or co-worker of a different race, or it may occur vicariously, through the media or other channels. Prior to this experience, we are in a precontact condition in which Whiteness is either invisible to us or denied as a significant element of our identity (Kivel, 1996). Griffin (1995) writes: "By ourselves, we weren't racial at all. We were just people. Uncolored" (p. 28). Never having met a person who wasn't White, I was in the precontact stage for the first 18 years of my life. In the contact stage we are usually uncomfortable and unsophisticated in our initial relationships with people of color. We are timid and naively curious. This was my experience on my first interracial date in high school, as described in Chapter 1. In the contact stage we often unconsciously exhibit stereotypical racist attitudes and behaviors, as I did in worrying about my safety in going into "her neighborhood" for a date.

Some White people in the contact stage espouse the theory of color-blindness (Neville, et al, 2000; Schofield, 2000) and make comments that appear to be racist to people of color, such as, "I don't recognize what race a person is" (Helms, 1990, p. 57). In the contact stage we do not see ourselves as being White, and we are unaware that people from other racial groups see us in particular ways because of our Whiteness. As Aileen Moreton-Robinson, one of my Aboriginal colleagues in Australia points out, "White people are often shocked to discover that Indigenous women think critically and have opinions about them" (Narratives). Likewise, Finefrock (Narratives) was surprised to learn that she was viewed as either "a narc, a prostitute, or a drug pusher" when she moved into a Black neighborhood as a single White woman. In the same vein, McKenna states, "I understood that one of the unearned privileges I enjoyed as a White man in our society included rarely, if ever, being forced to be aware of my race" (Narratives).

Whites in the contact stage are ignorant of White privilege and unaware of the benefits that come to us because of institutional and cultural racism. Following our initial encounters with people of color, we may feel pressure from our White peers to discontinue such relationships. When we do form a positive friendship with a person of color, we tend to see this person as an exception to our negative stereotypes about other members of that group. We may say to our friend, "You're not like the others" or "You're a credit to your race."

Disintegration. We enter the stage of disintegration when we acknowledge our Whiteness and begin to question what we have been socialized to believe about race. Gallagher (Narratives) writes: "My first year of teaching sent me down the road of questioning my attitudes and childhood tapes about those different from me." Through our growing awareness of racial inequality, we begin to recognize certain moral dilemmas regarding race and the democratic ideals we espouse (Dennis, 1981; Howard, 2002; Parker, 2003). Our belief in the American principles of life, liberty, and the pursuit of happiness, for example, come into conflict with our growing awareness of the unfair and unequal treatment afforded Blacks and other people of color. Our values regarding fair treatment of people as individuals collide with our new awareness that racial minorities are often treated negatively and unfairly merely because of their group membership.

In the disintegration stage we experience considerable dissonance regarding our Whiteness. We feel anxiety, guilt, or shame regarding the discrepancies between our expressed values and the realities of racial discrimination. Linton (Narratives), for example, felt shocked and guilty when she realized that the anger of Black youth toward Whites in the 1960s was also directed toward her as a White community worker, even though she was trying to help ease the tensions in their riot-torn neighborhood. Similarly, McKenna (Narratives) describes his confusion in the disintegration stage when he discovered as a high school student that racism related to housing existed in his own neighborhood. He writes in his narrative: "Race and racism were no longer things I talked about in the abstract. . . . The struggles Anne [his Black neighbor] talked about were very real. I failed to see them until they came knocking literally at my door. For quite awhile I felt broken, confused, guilty."

Confronted with the difficult emotions of the disintegration stage, we may begin to reevaluate our previous attitudes and values, or we may blame racial others for our confusion and become angry with them. We may also feel alienated from our White peers, friends, and families, who often respond negatively to us when we challenge or destroy White norms about race. Sweaney (Narratives) discovered this rejection by her fellow Whites when she and her husband became advocates for Aboriginal students in their small Australian country town. She writes: "As we began to publicly articulate what was happening in both the school and the town, we, too, became outsiders to the non-Aboriginal community."

In addition to feelings of rejection, alienation, and dissonance during the disintegration stage, we may also experience a sense of excitement, stimulation, and discovery because of our newfound learnings about racial differences. Our attempts to navigate the swirling emotional currents of the disintegration stage often cause us to seek out one of several alternative ways to calm the rough waters. Some Whites may choose to withdraw from future contact with people of color, thus eliminating one source of the dissonant input. Others may attempt to convince White friends that people of color aren't really as bad as we may have been taught. Still others may recruit support from both Whites and people of color to create the illusion that racism is not really as destructive as it may appear.

Reintegration. For some Whites, however, the dissonance and the dilemmas of the disintegration stage are resolved through regression to previously held prejudices and the reassertion of racist beliefs. This is called the reintegration stage, wherein individuals consciously embrace the notion of White superiority. From this perspective, racism and inequality are rationalized as the natural result of the inherent inferiority of people of color. The guilt and anxiety of the previous stage are repressed and redirected as fear or anger toward other racial groups. These emotions can be passively expressed by avoiding people of color and relating only to like-minded Whites, or they can be more actively asserted in the form of hostility and/or violence. Militias, the Ku Klux Klan, Neo-Nazis, and other White supremacist groups are fixated in the reintegration stage. Members of these groups are conscious of their Whiteness, they espouse and rationalize their racial superiority, and they actively support attitudes and behaviors that denigrate people of color.

Reintegration behaviors, however, are not always based on the obvious ignorance of these blatantly racist groups. For example, the supremacist passions that fired the imaginations of *The Bell Curve* authors (Herrnstein & Murray, 1994) and the more subtle paternalism espoused by those who penned *No Excuses* (Thernstrom & Thernstrom, 2003), clearly demonstrates the "higher-level racism" that is sometimes evident within the academic community. Similar reintegration behaviors were exposed in the corporate boardroom at Texaco in 1997, where high-level executives using derogatory racist language were tape-recorded in a private meeting. Also, the university-educated parents who attacked the REACH multicultural program (Chapter 4) espoused a Western supremacist ideology that was different in style, but identical in substance, to that of their more blatantly racist compatriots in the Klan.

Both the raw bigotry of the streets and the refined racism of the ivory tower thrive during the reintegration stage. Racism is more conscious and intentional here than during the precontact, contact, or disintegration stages. Reintegration, which might better be termed "retrenchment," occurs as Whites retreat from the dissonance of disintegration and consciously choose racism and White superiority as their means of dealing with diversity. Much of the conservative political response that has been characterized in the popular press as "White male backlash" can be attributed to the dynamics of the reintegration stage. Whites in reintegration often feel "beseiged" or "victimized" by people from other racial groups, whom they perceive as directing "reverse" racial discrimination against Whites (Giroux, 1997b, pp. 287–288). At this point in the developmental cycle, Whiteness is no longer invisible but is consciously acknowledged and actively defended against perceived outsiders. Whether their racism is covert or overt, it often requires powerful experiential influences to dislodge individuals who become fixated in the reintegration stage (Helms, 1990).

Pseudo-independence. Fortunately, there is an alternative to reintegration, which occurs when a White person "begins to question her or his previous definition of Whiteness and the justifiability of racism in any of its forms" (Helms, 1990, p. 61). The pseudo-independence stage begins when we acknowledge White responsibility for racism and confront the fact that White people have intentionally or unintentionally benefited from it. Our attempts to abandon racism in this stage are usually characterized by a desire to "help" people from other racial groups rather than to systematically change the dynamics of dominance. The missionary zeal of the pseudo-independence stage often grows from a conviction that Whites really do have the answers for other people. This stage was typified for me in my early work in the Black community in New Haven, where I saw myself as "helping Black kids survive the struggles of life in the ghetto." Because of a continuing belief in White moral superiority, individuals in the pseudo-independence stage are often viewed suspiciously by members of other racial groups.

In the pseudo-independence stage we are attempting to give up our negative feelings about Whiteness, but we have not yet established an authentic White racial and cultural identity. We have not discovered role models who demonstrate how we can be both White *and* nonracist. Some of us at this stage may seek to disavow our own Whiteness and become judgmental of other Whites who are not aware of their racism. This was my stage of growth when I worked in the church (Chapter 1). I wanted to convince members of my White congregation that they were racist and unaware. Needless to say, pseudo-independent Whites often feel alienated from other White people.

Whereas Blacks in the immersion/emersion stage sometimes seek to prove they are "Blacker-than-thou" relative to other African Americans, Whites in the pseudo-independence stage often try to demonstrate that we are "less-White-than-thou" relative to our White peers, thus distancing ourselves from other members of our own collective group. The confusion and struggle of the pseudo-independence stage are evidence that our growth toward a positive sense of Whiteness remains tentative and unfocused at this point in the developmental cycle. Most of our reexamination of Whiteness at this stage is occurring at the intellectual level, with the deeper emotional issues left unresolved.

Immersion/emersion. The transition into the immersion/emersion stage is marked by a movement away from paternalistic efforts to help other groups and toward an internalized desire to change oneself and one's fellow Whites in a positive way. For me, this stage marked the end of my "missionary period" in the Black community and the beginning of a genuine search for a new kind of White identity. Immersion/emersion is a "process of exploration and self-discovery" wherein the central question becomes, "How can I be proud of my race without being a racist?" (Carter, 1995, pp. 107–108). Similarly, Helms (1990) recognizes two important issues of this stage: "Who am I racially?" and "Who do I want to be?" (p. 62).

Whites in the immersion/emersion stage are on a quest for images and aspects of ourselves that are positive and unrelated to racism. We may join White consciousness-raising groups and seek out White role models who are antiracist allies. We want to associate with Whites who are on a similar journey, and we seek more authentic and proactive ways of being White. Much of the work at this stage is being done at the emotional level, sorting out and working through issues that were repressed, denied, or avoided in the earlier stages.

Autonomy. When a new and positive definition of Whiteness has been emotionally and intellectually internalized, we begin to enter the stage of autonomous racial identity. In this stage, according to Helms's model, race is no longer a threat to us. We have acknowledged the reality of personal, cultural, and institutional racism, and we are engaged in activities to resist the many manifestations of oppression (Howard, 2004; Tatum, 2003). Tatum (1992) writes:

> Alliances with people of color can be more easily forged at this stage of development than previously because the person's antiracist behaviors and attitudes will be more consistently expressed. (p. 339)

In the autonomy stage we begin to draw correlations and connections between racism and other forms of inequality and dominance, including sexism, heterosexism, classism, and ageism. We become clearer in our understanding that oppression in *all* of its forms ought to be the target of our social change initiatives. We actively seek opportunities to learn from other groups, and we are able to engage in authentic personal interactions across the boundaries of difference. It was from the position of autonomous White identity that Bob Conners (Narratives), as a White male professor, was able to honestly and effectively teach a class on racism and oppression in American society to a student population that was primarily Black.

In the Helms model, autonomy does not represent an end-point in the cycle of growth. It is not necessarily a transcendence of race, but rather a state of being continually open to new information and growth. In the autonomy stage, which I refer to in my work as the stage of authenticity, we acquire a new and positive connection to our Whiteness and a deep commitment to resist oppression. As one of Tatum's (1992) White students stated at the end of an intense term-long exploration of racial identity, "It was not being White that I was disavowing, but being racist" (p. 340).

CAUTIONARY NOTES

Helms's description of stages in the development of White racial identity, like any theoretical construct, is merely an approximation of actual experience. The chronology of growth implied by her model can be helpful as a guide and as an educative tool but may not be accurate or appropriate for everyone. In my own developmental process, for example, the reintegration stage was never a reality, and none of the White teachers who shared their stories in the Narratives seem to have entered this phase. Reintegration behaviors are certainly real, as discussed above, but it would be erroneous to assume that all White people necessarily pass through this stage.

Also, some White people share personal accounts in which they appear to have "skipped" several of the earlier stages of identity development, apparently having been acculturated into autonomous multicultural identity from early infancy. Wellman (1999), for example, tells of being raised by Communist parents in Detroit in the 1950s, where Black friends and house guests were more common than White ones. He grew up with the disparaging appellation of "red" rather than White, and felt much safer in the racially diverse milieu of his parents' political activism than he did in predominantly White settings. He writes, "The White teachers treated me no differently than my Black classmates: suspiciously, and sometimes with contempt. Whatever privileges Whiteness conferred were cancelled by my redness" (p. 79). Wellman's story exudes images of immersion/emersion and autonomy/authenticity but lacks references to the earlier stages. His narrative is a reminder that we should avoid being either too literal or too linear in our application of racial identity theories.

It is also important to note that research related to White racial identity is a relatively recent phenomenon, gaining momentum only in the 1990s. Even though Whiteness has become a major topic of study in recent years (Allen, 1999; C. Clark & O'Donnell, 1999; Howard, 2004; Johnson, 2001; Leach et al., 2002; Rodriguez & Villaverde, 2000; Weiss & Fine, 2003; Wise, 2003) it should be acknowledged that our understanding of the process of White identity development is still tentative and exploratory. Some researchers claimed even by the late 1990s that enough had already been written about Whiteness. They worried that "understanding Whiteness could surface as the new intellectual fetish, leaving questions of power, privilege, and race/ethnic political minorities behind as an intellectual 'fad' of the past" (Fine et al., 1997, p. xii).

I find it encouraging, rather than worrisome, that more researchers have begun to examine Whiteness and that White educators are now sharing their narratives regarding the personal struggles related to racial identity development. I feel we need to deepen and expand our work on Whiteness rather than terminate it in its initial stages. The examination of Whiteness is an essential, and formerly neglected, part of the broader multicultural and social justice agenda. As I have argued throughout this book, we cannot begin to dismantle the legacy of dominance without first engaging Whites in a deep analysis of our own role in perpetuating injustice. We need to decode White dominance and also provide ourselves and our White colleagues with positive visions for engaging in the process of change (Giroux, 1997a). To this end, the current discussion of White racial identity are only now beginning to manifest their potential contribution. We need more work in this arena, not less.

In spite of these cautions and concerns, however, the value of a positive developmental approach to White racial identity lies in its emphasis on growth and the possibility of change. By establishing racial identity as a process of development, rather than a fixed and immutable attribute, these theories offer hope for the process of social healing. As White educators working in multicultural settings, we are indebted to Helms, Tatum, Carter, Sleeter, and other theorists who have initiated work in the field of White racial identity development. Although they do not answer all our questions regarding the dilemmas and confusions of White racial identity, their emerging conceptual frameworks certainly help us map the major steps along the way. Just as Erikson's life-cycle formulations were comforting for me during my identity turmoil in the 1960s, so the stages of White racial identity development can lend legitimacy and worthiness to the challenges and frustrations we inevitably face in our growth toward an authentic and transformationist White identity, a process I will explore in more depth in the following chapter.

CHAPTER 6

Ways of Being White: A Practitioner's Approach to Multicultural Growth

When Whiteness is discussed in educational settings, the emphasis is almost exclusively on revealing it as an ideology of privilege mediated largely through the dynamics of racism. While such interventions are crucial in developing an anti-racist pedagogy, they do not go far enough.

—Henry Giroux, "Rewriting the Discourse of Racial Identity"

My friends and colleagues from other racial groups often tease me about "acting White," particularly when I become overly concerned with details and time constraints. I usually take these jibes in the light-hearted way they are intended, but I also want to challenge the assumption that "acting White" has any consistent or singular meaning. Theories of White racial identity development clearly demonstrate there is more than one way of being White. "Acting White" can have multiple and even contradictory meanings, depending on a given White person's stage of racial identity development. As we saw in the previous chapter, each stage describes a significantly different approach to issues of race and Whiteness. A White person in the reintegration/retrenchment stage, for example, is consciously racist, whereas an individual in the stage of autonomy/authenticity is actively antiracist. A person in the disintegration stage is confused and conflicted about his or her own Whiteness, whereas an individual in autonomy/authenticity has evolved a positive cultural and racial identity. Because of these differences, there is no single way of "acting White," and Whites in one stage of identity development often experience conflict with their White peers in other stages.

This potential for conflict was illustrated when one of our recently certified REACH national trainers went home to share her multicultural knowledge with relatives over the Thanksgiving holiday. She distributed workshop handouts, put the overhead projector on the dining room table, and invited her parents and siblings to experience a few multicultural training activities. Unfortunately, her mini-workshop lasted no longer than the first transparency, which presented the concept of "multiple perspectives." Her father quickly grew irritated and challenged her basic premise that other cultures have valid perspectives to offer Whites. A verbal donnybrook ensued, from which it was difficult to salvage a modicum of fellowship for the turkey dinner. This was our trainer's last attempt to share her newfound multicultural knowledge with the folks back home. She was in the stage of pseudo-independence at the time, enthusiastic in her efforts to convince other Whites of their lack of awareness. Her father was instantly catapulted into reintegration, with all of the resistance and denial characteristic of that stage. In this situation, the father and daughter were each manifesting their Whiteness in entirely different ways.

Recognizing that educators represent a broad range of different stages in our racial identity development, my wife, Dr. Lotus Linton, and I became interested in mapping the process of multicultural growth. Beginning in 1989 we initiated a process that engaged educators and other professionals in a series of weekend seminars and dialogues designed to explore the deeper dimensions of personal and professional growth relative to racial and cultural diversity. Our intent was not only to describe the significant experiences and guideposts along the path of development but also to determine how we might encourage and stimulate such growth in other educators. Four assumptions guided our work:

1. Growth in multicultural awareness is possible.
2. Growth in multicultural awareness is desirable.
3. Multicultural growth can be observed and assessed.
4. Multicultural growth can be stimulated and promoted.

From our initial work with educators in several intensive seminars over a three-year period, we developed a model of multicultural growth. The model has subsequently been revised and adapted by the REACH Center, and utilized by our staff and national trainers with thousands of workshop participants throughout the United States and Australia since the early 1990s.

WHITE IDENTITY ORIENTATIONS

For the purpose of this book, I have built upon previous work with my wife and the REACH Center and created a model that relates specifically to different ways of being White. The model, as presented in the accompanying chart in Table 6.1, recognizes three distinct White identity orientations, which I have designated as fundamentalist, integrationist, and transformationist White identity. Each orientation is described by nine indicators, which are, in turn, clustered into three modalities of growth, including thinking, feeling, and acting. Each orientation is profoundly different from the others in terms of (1) how Whites *think* relative to the constructs of truth, Whiteness, and dominance; (2) how Whites *feel* relative to self-awareness, racial differences, and discussions of racism; and (3) how Whites *act* relative to teaching, management, and cross-cultural interactions.

The White identity orientations model provides a means of tracking how White educators can progress in our thoughts, emotions, and behaviors relative to Whiteness and issues of dominance. I offer the model as a way to support, extend, and complement the work of other researchers and practitioners who have developed theories of White racial identity development. I present the White orientations model not as a fully developed theory but rather as a conceptual tool that has grown from many years of engagement with White educators in the process of multicultural identity development. It is a practitioner's model, designed to further describe and clarify the different ways of being White. My hope in presenting the White orientations model is that it will facilitate and encourage the process of growth toward greater multicultural competence among White educators. In the discussion that follows, I describe each of the orientations and share stories that illustrate how individual White educators have grown from one orientation to the next.

Fundamentalist White Identity

Thinking. Fundamentalist Whites are literal and linear thinkers regarding issues of race and Whiteness. They are fixed and rigid in their cognitive functioning and immutably committed, either consciously or unconsciously, to the assumption of White supremacy. A White person in the fundamentalist orientation adheres to the single-dimensional understanding of truth that is characteristic of all forms of fundamentalism. Fundamentalist Whites are zealous defenders of the single-truth reality that "White is right." They shun ambiguity. White dominance is rationalized, legitimized, and actively perpetuated. In its less intentional and more unconscious form, fundamentalist White thinking may be characterized by denial and/or ignorance of Whiteness and White supremacy. Unaware fundamentalist Whites often do not see themselves as racial beings at all but prefer to describe themselves as "just American" or "just Australian."

Table 6.1. White Identity Orientations

WHITE IDENTITY ORIENTATIONS

MODALITIES OF GROWTH	FUNDAMENTALIST	INTEGRATIONIST	TRANSFORMATIONIST
Construction of Truth	Literal and fixed Single-dimensional truth Western-centric	Acknowledge diverse perspectives Interest in broader truths Continued defense of Western superiority	Legitimacy of diverse perspectives Truth as dynamic/changing Actively seeking divergent truths
Construction of Whiteness	Supremacist/White is right Ignorance/avoidance Confusion	Beginning awareness Some self-interrogation Dissonance	Self-reflective critique Deep interrogation of Whiteness Affirming authentic/positive/nonracist identity
Construction of Dominance	Legitimize/perpetuate dominance Rationalize Deny/ignore	Victim's perspective Personal rather than institutional critique of dominance	Acknowledge complicity Holistic critique of oppression Comprehensive analysis of dominance
Level of Self-Awareness	My perspective is right – the only one Self-esteem linked to supremacy Threatened by differences	My perspective is one of many Self-esteem linked to "helping" others "Wannabe" phenomenon	My perspective is changing Self-esteem linked to growth and change I am enhanced by connection to different groups
Emotional Response to Differences	Fear/hostility/avoidance Judgment Colorblindness	Interest Beginning awareness Cultural voyeurism/curiosity	Appreciation/respect Enthusiasm/joy Honesty
Emotional Response to Discussions of Racism	Anger Denial Defensiveness/avoidance	Shame/guilt/confusion Missionary zeal Externalized as someone else's problem	Acknowledgment/empathy Enlightened aversion to oppression Responsibility without guilt
Approach to Cross-Cultural Interactions	Distance/isolation Hostility Reinforcing White superiority	Narrowly circumscribed/tentative Patronizing Emphasizing commonalities	Active seeking Deeply personal/rewarding Transforming/healing
Approach to Teaching About Differences	Monocultural 'Treat all students "the same"' Actively Eurocentric	Special program for special folks Learning about other cultures Tacitly Eurocentric	Social action/authentic engagement Learning from other cultures Challenging the Eurocentric perspective
Approach to Leadership/Management	Autocratic/directive Assimilationist Perpetuates White dominance	Compliance oriented Invite others into "our" house Tacit support of White dominance	Advocacy Collaboration/co-responsibility Challenging/dismantling White dominance

Feeling. Relative to the feeling modality, fundamentalist Whites harbor a strong emotional commitment to the rightness of their own perspective. Their self-esteem is bolstered by the assumption of White superiority. People from different races and cultures, or other White people who espouse different definitions of truth, are responded to with fear, hostility, or avoidance. Some well-meaning fundamentalist Whites may be emotionally committed to a belief in colorblindness, which allows them to deny and avoid differences (Chapter 3). When confronted with the issue of their own racism, individuals in this orientation respond with anger, denial, or defensiveness.

Acting. Whites in the fundamentalist orientation are either overtly or covertly racist in their cross-cultural interactions. The more overt fundamentalist Whites are hostile toward people of different races and they usually seek to avoid such encounters whenever possible. The more covert, or well-intentioned, fundamentalists Whites often claim that they do not see differences or that they treat all students "the same." Fundamentalist White educators demonstrate a monocultural and Eurocentric approach to teaching. Their curriculum content and pedagogy reflect an inherent commitment to Western supremacy. They resist multicultural education and pride themselves on preaching an assimilationist doctrine to their students of color. Fundamentalist Whites in positions of leadership are autocratic, directive, and committed to the preservation of White hegemony. They are ardent defenders of "business as usual" in those organizations that have traditionally been White-dominated.

Whites with a fundamentalist racial identity demonstrate a high degree of "social dominance orientation," which Sidanius and Pratto (1993) define as "the degree to which people desire and strive for superiority of the ingroup over the outgroup and oppose egalitarianism" (p. 178). This aspect of the fundamentalist White orientation was epitomized for me in a workshop I conducted with 25 White male school superintendents in Texas. I began the session by eliciting their concerns and issues regarding racial and cultural differences in their schools. One superintendent received broad approval from his peers when he said, "We know that Anglo culture is superior, but we can't figure out how to get our Black and Hispanic students and families to buy into it." These men were angry that parents should demand culturally relevant content and bilingual instruction. They resented having to attend my multicultural workshop. Their thinking modality was fixated on White supremacy; their feeling modality was locked into denial, hostility, and avoidance; and their acting modality was committed to an autocratic and monocultural defense of business-as-usual in the schools. I spent eight hours working with these gentlemen but was unable to make even the slightest dent in their White fundamentalist armor.

Changing. Powerful experiential catalysts are required to dislodge individuals from their fixation in the fundamentalist White orientation. Finefrock (Narratives) described one such experience in her relationship with two Black women who taught her about "the other side of the tracks" regarding race relations in her small Ohio town. Through their "wisdom, honesty, insight, and patience" these two powerful role models were able to dismantle the "bubble world of assumptions" that had been Finefrock's previous reality. Similarly, the mentoring I received from Black youth and community leaders in New Haven in the 1960s caused me to reorient my entire social reality and grow beyond the White fundamentalism of my youth (Chapter 1).

In another example of personal change, a young White professor in Australia, who had never previously grappled with diversity issues, became deeply unsettled in a recent workshop in Brisbane when he heard several stories of injustice told by women, immigrants, and Aboriginal participants. Following my presentation on the dominance paradigm, in which I shared the "fish discovering water" image (Chapter 3), he was obviously upset and said to me, "I feel like one of those fish who just discovered water, and I can't breathe. I have been living in dominance my whole life. I've been blind to so many issues, and I am amazed at how narrow my perspective has been. I now wonder how many of my previous assumptions are actually untrue."

Over the course of a three-day workshop, this young professor's fundamentalist White orientation gradually began to come apart. He was a willing participant in its demise, yet he also experienced considerable personal confusion and disorientation as his worldview slowly shifted to a more nuanced and multidimensional configuration. I was impressed with his honesty in confronting the new information, and I appreciated the example he set for other White participants who were also struggling with shifts in their own White identity orientations. He listened to the stories of racial "others," heard the message beneath the words, and had the courage to begin the process of personal change.

Integrationist White Identity

Thinking. The integrationist orientation represents a significant shift in thinking away from the fundamentalist perspective. Unlike their fundamentalist peers, integrationist Whites are willing to acknowledge the existence and legitimacy of diverse approaches to truth. Their acceptance of differences, however, is often rather shallow, and they prefer to think that "we're really all the same under the skin." Integrationists have begun the process of interrogating Whiteness, yet they remain ambivalent in their conclusions. They acknowledge the historical reality of White dominance, but they usually fail to grasp the significance of its continuing effects in contemporary social institutions. Because their assessment of racial issues is only skin deep, they often underestimate the depth of the change that will be necessary to achieve real equity and social justice.

For the most part, integrationist Whites see injustice as the victims' problem. As Sleeter (1994) points out, "We are willing to critique the psychological impact of slavery on Blacks, but not its impact on ourselves" (p. 6). Integrationist thinking does not question the legitimacy of Western hegemony and does not acknowledge the need for fundamental shifts in White consciousness. Although differences are acknowledged, a tacit acceptance of White superiority remains. Integrationist Whites are aware of the personal pain others have experienced because of White dominance, but they have not yet grasped the systemic and institutional nature of social inequality.

Feeling. In the affective domain, integrationist Whites have grown beyond the knee-jerk defensiveness of the fundamentalist orientation. Their positive self-regard now includes an interest in other cultures and races. They are curious about differences but often take a tourist's approach to learning about other racial and ethnic groups, sometimes verging on cultural voyeurism. They can become entangled in the emotions of the "wannabe" phenomenon, searching for their own identity in the images of other groups.

Integrationist Whites often demonstrate the emotional confusion, ambivalence, and dissonance associated with Helms' disintegration stage of identity development. Although they have acknowledged their complicity in racism at the intellectual and collective levels, they continue to distance themselves from racism at the personal and emotional levels. Feelings of racial superiority still linger, but they are more subtle and unconscious than in the fundamentalist orientation. Integrationist Whites can easily become embroiled in guilt, shame, or denial when directly confronted with their own personal racism. As Sleeter (1996) describes, "We . . . want confirming evidence from people of color that we are not racist, and many of us are afraid of saying something wrong that might undermine our 'non-racist' self-perception" (p. 22).

Acting. Integrationist Whites are open to cross-racial interactions, but their relationships with people from different groups are often narrowly

circumscribed and not deeply personal. They are most comfortable with
people of color who have achieved success in the dominant culture and do
not challenge Whites' assumptions about the inherent goodness of Western
hegemony (thus the popularity among some Whites of public figures such
as Clarence Thomas and Condoleezza Rice). White integrationist teachers
take an additive and contributions approach to multicultural education (J.
A. Banks, 1994). They want to teach about other cultures but tend to position their efforts as "special programs for special folks."

Leaders and managers in the integrationist orientation attempt to respond positively to diversity, but they are primarily concerned with issues
of compliance and assimilation rather than fundamental change or real
inclusion. Demonstrating the "quaint liberalism" (Giroux, 1997a, p. 237)
of this orientation, integrationist White managers are often paternalistic in
their interactions with people from different ethnic and racial groups, seeing
their White leadership role as one of "helping others." As an Aboriginal doctoral candidate in an Australian university, Moreton-Robinson (Narratives)
experienced this integrationist behavior from her White professors and su-
pervisors, who related to her paternalistically as an inferior "other," not as
an articulate and self-empowered Indigenous woman.

Integrationist leaders and teachers are well-meaning in their attempts
to respond to issues of difference, but they have neither deconstructed
dominance nor confronted their own White privilege. These aspects of the
integrationist perspective were exemplified in a discussion of "minority
scholarships" that took place among the faculty and administrators at a
prestigious private school in the Seattle area. A friend who teaches there
reported that the dominant perspective among her colleagues was expressed in the following way: "We don't need scholarships for children of
color because race is merely an abstraction." This sentiment is the ultimate
expression of White privilege. It is typical of the pseudo-sophistication
that is characteristic of the integrationist orientation. Although it is true,
from a purely scientific point of view, that race is a socially constructed
abstraction, racism and White dominance are realities that continue to diminish access to elite private school education for children of color. Race
may be a myth, but racism is real.

Exemplifying the luxury of ignorance and the privilege of social distance, integrationist Whites in this school were able to avoid the real issues of dominance by failing to question the basic assumptions that have
maintained their exclusionary practices. They did so by capitulating to
a supposedly "higher-order" intellectual understanding of race, one that
dismissed them from any responsibility to explore strategies for more effective outreach to students of color.

An Australian Aboriginal colleague, Bob Morgan, who served for many years as a high-ranking administrator in a large urban university in Sydney, has helped me gain a deeper understanding of the integrationist White orientation. Throughout most of Australia's history, Aboriginal people have been intentionally excluded from higher education, a product of the country's fundamentalist White orientation, officially known as the "White Australia Policy," which was in effect until the late 1960s and lingers on in many ways even today. Only recently have Aboriginal students been actively recruited to attend universities. Morgan and many other Aboriginal and White educators have worked diligently to help build supportive structures that will encourage Aboriginal students to persevere and succeed in these primarily White institutions. He says, "We have now been invited to the party, but the university is still *their* house. Only when the institution reflects and honors Aboriginal culture and clearly belongs to *all* of us will we feel fully included." As Finefrock says (Narratives), "We have a pronoun problem." From the perspective of the integrationist orientation, "we" refers to Whites and "they" refers to the people of color who are invited into "our" schools, institutions, and neighborhoods. For integrationist Whites, the racial and ethnic composition of the guests may change, but the rules of the house remain the same.

Changing. The integrationist orientation begins to break down when Whites realize that the "we" of our social institutions must be truly inclusive. This realization leads to the gradual disintegration of a Eurocentric and Western-dominated perspective. This transition happened for me in New Haven when I began to see that the purpose of my work was not to "help" Black youth or "save" the Black community, but rather to reeducate my fellow Whites and help dismantle the dominance paradigm in the White community. My focus shifted away from externalizing racism as someone else's problem and toward internalizing the issue of White racism as the fundamental focus of change.

In the process of growing beyond my integrationist orientation, it was necessary for me to become self-reflective regarding White dominance. Liz Sweaney, from her experience in an outback Australian school, documents a similar shift:

> We began to discern that the current practices and curriculum had little relevance to the majority of our [Aboriginal] students or, in fact, to ourselves. Although unspoken, we formed an alliance and I think became advocates for change. (Sweaney, Narratives)

The integrationist orientation can be transcended only when Whites begin to question the legitimacy of those institutional arrangements that continue to perpetuate White dominance. When Whites form alliances with people who have historically been marginalized by White hegemony, we ourselves become agents of change within the White community. When White paternalism is abandoned in the service of meaningful social action, we begin to disengage from the integrationist stance and move toward a transformationist orientation.

Transformationist White Identity

Thinking. Transformationist Whites actively seek to understand diverse points of view. They know that the construction of truth is a dynamic process that is continually shifting in the context of diverse cultural perspectives. They are aware that their personal appropriation of truth is merely one of many possibilities, not the *only* one. They are comfortable with multidimensional realities. Transformationist Whites challenge the legitimacy of White dominance. They welcome the process of self-interrogation that inevitably destabilizes their own assumptions about the commonplace and the normal (Fiske, 1989; Johnson, 2001). They acknowledge the collective reality of White complicity in dominance and oppression, while at the same time claiming a positive connection to White racial and cultural identity. Through their willingness to probe the deeper terrain of racial identity, they become self-reflective, authentic, and antiracist in their understanding of Whiteness.

Feeling. Transformationist Whites have abandoned the tacit assertion of White supremacy that lingers in the emotional backwaters of the integrationist orientation. Their personal pride and sense of self are no longer tied to assumptions of superiority but are grounded in the self-generated process of growth and learning. They affirm a positive sense of White identity, often finding a renewed and deep connection to their cultural roots in Europe. Transformationist Whites welcome the personal growth that continues to be generated by their exposure to diverse cultural realities. Their lives are enhanced rather than threatened by differences. They are guided by empathy and respect in their emotional response to people from different racial and cultural groups. Very importantly, their empathy also extends to other White people who have not grown as far as they have in their racial identity development. Transformationist Whites choose to assist their White colleagues in the process of growth rather than judging them for their inadequacies. Because they have worked through their own emotional issues of guilt and shame related to White racism and oppression, they do not need to project blame onto their White colleagues. Rather than being immobilized by the weight of history and the pain of dominance, they are motivated by a vision of healing and social justice.

Acting. White educators in the transformationist orientation are committed to social action for the purpose of dismantling the dominance paradigm. As they participate in the process of liberation for others, they acknowledge that they themselves are being liberated as well (Bishop, 1994). Mutual growth and the commitment to change are essential for becoming allies in this work (Kivel, 1996). Transformationist Whites realize they cannot dismantle White dominance without fundamentally altering their own White identity. In a profound understatement, Sleeter (1996) notes that "becoming actively involved in working to dismantle racism will change a person's life" (p. 26).

Transformationist Whites actively seek cross-cultural and cross-racial interactions because they realize their own growth is dependent on such connections. Likewise, they engage their students in a continuous process of exploring multiple perspectives. As my wife found in her experience as a teacher in inner-city schools, transformationist Whites enjoy learning *from* and *with* other cultures, rather than merely *about* them (Linton, Narratives). Transformationist White teachers create curricula that manifest a multidimensional view of reality, and their pedagogy fosters equity, inclusion, and empowerment for all their students (J. A. Banks & C.A.M. Banks, 2005).

Transformationist White leaders and managers are champions of healing and change. They are advocates for those people who have been marginalized by the forces of dominance and oppression. They actively interrogate institutional structures, policies, and procedures. They are self-reflective regarding their own leadership style, seeking to be collaborative and co-responsible in their approach to change.

Changing. Whites who enter the transformationist orientation have experienced a profound shift in their understanding of the world and themselves. They have acknowledged, critiqued, and rejected the legitimacy of the dominance paradigm. They have committed themselves to a lifelong process of dismantling the assumption of rightness, the luxury of ignorance, and the legacy of privilege that have been the foundations of White hegemony for centuries. Although there is no ultimate escape from these negative realities of Whiteness, they are not overwhelmed by guilt or shame. Having changed themselves, they are passionate about educating other Whites and committed to working with colleagues from all racial groups to overcome the social arrangements of past and present dominance.

For transformationist Whites, the privileges of avoidance and non-engagement have been significantly eroded. Almojuela, a Native American colleague, told me recently:

> I used to think that Whites in social justice work always had the privilege of leaving when things got too uncomfortable for them. Whereas this is probably true for many, I now see that there are some White people who have gone too far down the road of commitment to turn back. Their hearts and minds are too deeply engaged in the healing work for them to leave it. There is no choice for them. This was a profound thing for me to realize because I never looked at Whites in this way before.

Almojuela's insight is echoed by one of Nieto's (1998) White students who, after learning many lessons about Whiteness in the context of an intense multicultural discussion group, said in her final report, "Now I can never *not* know again" (p. 20). Similarly, Sweaney (Narratives) comments of her 10 years of transformational work with Aboriginal students in a racist country town in Australia: "I found this time to be the most challenging, exciting, creative, and constructive in my career. I grew not only as a teacher, but also as a person. What I gained from the friendships made has become a part of my very being."

As inspirational as these words might be, it is important not to romanticize the transformationist White orientation as an end-point in the journey to cultural and racial awareness. Transformationist identity is, in itself, an ongoing process of change and growth. At the same time, it is helpful and hopeful for White educators to realize that there are different ways of being White and that we have a choice and an opportunity to grow beyond the limits of either the fundamentalist or integrationist orientations. It is also important to acknowledge that it may be too early in our exploration of White identity formation to more rigorously prescribe the best methodology whereby we might achieve positive movement for ourselves, our colleagues, and our students. The White identity orientations model, however, does provide a tentative roadmap to guide our growth in the three modalities of thinking, feeling, and acting. By critically analyzing dominance, by exploring possibilities for emotional growth, and by creating new arenas of collaborative and transformative action, there is much we can do to encourage our White colleagues and students to join us on the road to social justice, healing, and positive racial identity. The actual work of transformationist White teachers in the classroom will be the focus of the next chapter.

REFLECTIONS ON THE RHETORIC OF WHITENESS

Before leading a workshop with middle school teachers in North Carolina, my training partner and I were informed by school district administrators that our prospective audience of educators had been highly resistant in previous multicultural inservice sessions. Teachers resented being forced to attend these workshops. They had verbally attacked previous presenters and had once even stormed out of the room in mass protest. We were not comforted by this information, which was shared with us just minutes before our session began.

We worked with this group of 60 teachers in North Carolina for a full day and were both surprised and impressed by their positive attitude and willingness to engage in the various discussions and activities that we introduced. We dealt with issues of multicultural curriculum infusion, and also with the realities of prejudice, power, and racism in their schools. We did not attempt to compensate for the alleged recalcitrance of our audience, but merely tried to be inclusive in our approach and open to their perspectives. At the end of the session, one of the more senior faculty members, a White woman who had worked in this school district for 25 years, came up to thank us. She said, "This is the tenth multicultural workshop I have been to in the past few years, and it's the first time I haven't felt blamed. Thank you for treating me like a professional."

In another instance, Nieto (1998) shares a journal entry from one of her White male students at the end of a term-long discussion of racial issues in a highly interactive and diverse setting with other students. Her student wrote:

> I still do not accept the definition of racism that "if you are White in America, you have benefited and are therefore a racist." This guilt-laden definition is great for provoking response, but in my opinion is simplistic, divisive, and more importantly, could completely discourage adherents from seeking change. The definition itself is racist, or at least too "pat." (pp. 28–29)

Both the teacher in North Carolina and the student in Nieto's class remind us to exercise care in our rhetorical formulations, lest we fall victim to the very exclusion and stereotyping we are attempting to dismantle. The rhetoric of blame and guilt often pushes our White students and colleagues into the stage of perpetual reintegration, locking them into resistance and self-protection rather than responsible reflection and positive growth. If we want to engage the issues of White dominance and racism in a compelling way, then we must allow for open dialogue and the possibility of change. We must learn to use the language of discovery and exploration, rather than the rhetoric of blame and projection. We must continually invite our White colleagues to see the potential for their role as allies in the work of social healing.

Since the first edition of this book was published in 1999, the study of Whiteness has become a virtual cottage industry in the academic community. Scores of graduate students and academics have asked me for permission to use the White identity orientations model in their dissertations and research. As more scholarly attention becomes focused on Whiteness and White racial identity development, it is important to consider the political and educational implications of this relatively new arena of research. We need to clarify our use of language and vigilantly assess the rhetoric that frames our discussion of Whiteness. If our intention is to be inclusive, then it is essential that our interrogation of Whiteness not be confined to the academic community but be made accessible to a broad audience of educational practitioners.

I raise these concerns as a multicultural practitioner who has worked with many teachers in schools throughout the United States and Australia over the past 40 years. In multicultural teacher training, as in any other educational endeavor, our pedagogical approach ought to be developmentally appropriate for the audience we are attempting to reach. Rather than blaming unaware White teachers for the sins of past dominance, we need to start where they are, which for many White teachers means dealing with the earlier stages of White identity development, including precontact, contact, disintegration, and reintegration. When we employ the language of blame and guilt with Whites who are in these early stages of development, we essentially contribute to the perpetuation of the very denial and resistance we are attempting to overcome. To this end, it is important to remember that the "enemies" in our multicultural healing work are dominance, ignorance, and racism, not White people. "Affirmation before reformation" is as important in our work with White teachers as it is in our work with children (Geneva Gay, personal communication, March 1997).

In light of the above discussion, I worry about the use of academic rhetoric that equates Whiteness with oppression. Sleeter (1996), for example, states that "Whiteness has come to mean ravenous materialism, competitive individualism, and a way of living characterized by putting acquisition of possession ahead of humanity" (p. 31). Fine and colleagues (1997) similarly claim that "Whiteness demands and constitutes hierarchy, exclusion, and deprivation" (p. viii). In addition, Roediger (1994) writes that "it is not merely that Whiteness is oppressive and false; it is nothing but oppressive and false" (p. 13). And with perhaps the most extreme rhetorical flourish, Ignatiev (1996) claims that "the key to solving the social problems of our time is to abolish the White race" (p. 10).

Whereas it is essential to acknowledge, as I did in Chapters 2 and 3, the inherent connection between oppression and Whiteness, it is equally important to critically examine the scholarly rhetoric employed in our attempts to deconstruct Whiteness. We must carefully seek to understand the implications of our rhetoric for the healing work of social justice and personal transformation. From a practitioner's point of view, I am concerned that the analytical approach of "Whiteness-equals-oppression" will merely serve to alienate White educators rather than inspire them to become co-responsible for positive change.

If Whiteness is theorized to be synonymous with oppression, then how do we provide White educators with a positive racial identity and include them in the work of social transformation? When writers in the "Whiteness-equals-oppression" genre wish to free White people from their own definitional constraints, they are forced to exercise further rhetorical sleight-of-hand by differentiating between "White people" and "Whiteness." Thus Sleeter (1996) writes: "To break with Whiteness, I must first distinguish between being a person of European ancestry and one who identifies with being 'White'" (p. 32). This careful distinction may function well in theory but raises significant problems for educational practice (Giroux, 1997b).

No matter how unbecoming my Whiteness may be made to appear, I cannot "un-become" White. Given the common use of language and the real politics of race, I am both White and European American. I cannot separate "Whiteness" from "being White" from "being of European ancestry." Any attempt to do so is merely a word game. As Delpit (1995) has cautioned, the language we employ in the deconstruction of Whiteness often functions "not for the purpose of better teaching, but for the goal of easier analysis" (p. 46). Relative to the stages of racial identity development, the "Whiteness-equals-oppression" rhetoric emerges from the kind of self-loathing that is often associated with the disintegration stage as well as from the "less-White-than-thou" attitude that is characteristic of pseudo-independence.

Regardless of any rhetorical distinctions we may employ, White educators and students will continue to be seen as White. As McKenna (Narratives) learned from his early struggles as a teacher in predominantly Black schools, "As much as I despised Whiteness, that is what I was." The goal for White people in the process of racial identity development is not to un-become White but rather to transform for ourselves, and hopefully for others, the *meaning* of Whiteness. If Whiteness is by definition bad, then so are White people. Telling White people not to identify with Whiteness is tantamount to telling Black people not to identify with Blackness. It is an invitation to deny one's very existence.

Our attempts to dismantle dominance and oppression must follow a path other than that of either villifying or obliterating Whiteness. Just as African Americans have challenged the negative associations of "Blackness" and chosen to recast their identity in their own positive image, so Whites need to acknowledge and work through the negative historical implications of "Whiteness" and create for ourselves a transformed identity as White people committed to equity and social change. Our goal is to neither deify nor denigrate Whiteness, but to defuse its destructive power. To teach my White students and my own White children and grandchildren that they are "not White" is to do them a disservice. However, to teach them that there are different ways of being White, and that they have a *choice* as White people to become champions of justice and social healing, is to provide them a positive direction for growth and to grant them the dignity of their own being.

CHAPTER 7

White Teachers and School Reform: Toward a Transformationist Pedagogy

> Often, without knowing it, we are waiting for a new idea to come and cut us free from our entanglements. When the idea is true and the space is ready for it, the idea overtakes everything. With grace-like swiftness, it descends and claims recognition; it cannot be returned or reversed.
>
> —John O'Donohue, *Beauty*

What is the new idea we have been waiting for that will free us from the entanglements of White dominance and the tragic persistence of educational inequities for children of color in our public schools? Since the first edition of this book was published in 1999, I have worked with tens of thousands of educators in school districts and universities throughout the United States. For the most part, the core content of these sessions has centered on the conversation we have engaged in here: How do we prepare a predominantly White teacher population to work effectively with racially and culturally diverse students? The conversation has become increasingly intense and more politically strident over the years, with issues of the achievement gap, high-stakes testing, school reform, and the federal No Child Left Behind legislation taking center stage.

In this chapter, I will use the current climate in public education as a backdrop onto which we can project, focus, and illuminate the two central themes we have discussed in the previous chapters: (1) the dynamics of White social dominance and (2) the developmental process whereby White educators grow toward a transformationist racial identity. It is from these two themes that we can forge the new idea that will help extricate us from the restraints of the past. And the new idea which emerges from this

book is that those of us who have benefited from the history of White privilege do not have to perpetuate it into the next generation. We, through our
consciousness and our commitment to social justice, can choose to direct
our power, our personhood, and our profession toward the erosion and
eventual extinction of White dominance. As educators, this healing work
begins in the schools. In this chapter I will show what we as transformationist White teachers *know* about our practice, what we *do* in our classrooms, and how we can and do make positive and healing contributions
everyday in countless ways in our nation's schools.

SOCIAL DOMINANCE AND THE ACHIEVEMENT GAP

We begin by revisiting the discussion of social dominance presented in
Chapters 2 and 3 and using this conceptual framework as a lens through
which to understand the existence and persistence of the achievement
gap. Transformationist White educators know that the achievement gap
cannot be understood without honestly confronting issues of social dominance. The process of schooling is neither power-neutral, race-neutral,
nor culture-neutral (Kozol, 2005; Noguera, 2003). It is no mere coinci-
dence that the children of certain racial, cultural, linguistic, and economic
groups—those who have for centuries been marginalized by the force of
Western White domination—are the same students who are now failing
or underachieving at disproportionate rates in our nation's schools. The
race-based achievement gap in public education today *is* the demographic embodiment of our history of White social, political, and economic
dominance.

Even though we have now commemorated the 50th anniversary of
the historic 1954 *Brown v. Board of Education* decision that declared *dejure*
racial segregation in schools unconstitutional, it is clear that educational
access has not led to educational *success* for vast numbers of our nation's
youth (Gay, 2000; Nieto, 2004; Noguera, 2003). Schooling, like all other
social institutions, continues to function as a system of privilege and preference, reinforced by power, favoring certain groups over others. Racial
separation continues to be deeply entrenched in our nation's schools, with
White students being the most racially segregated group (Kozol, 2005;
Orfield & Eaton, 1996). This is the sad asymmetry of social dominance:
The victors of history disproportionately thrive while the descendents of
the vanquished struggle just to survive. Such inequities are perpetuated
through the same three highly interrelated and mutually reinforcing dynamics of dominance that we have discussed in Chapter 3: the assumption
of rightness, the luxury of ignorance, and the legacy of privilege. We will

examine here how each of these is intrinsically tied to the perpetuation of the achievement gap. This is a level of analysis in which we, as transformationist White educators, must engage if we are to be effective in our work for social justice in our nation's schools. It is this analysis that tells us why the mere integration of schools has not led to full educational equity for children of color and other marginalized groups.

The assumption of rightness, as related to the achievement gap, often leads teachers to assume that the problem of school failure lies in the students and their families and not in the structure or function of schooling. We make assumptions about who can and cannot learn, and the more uncomfortable we are with difference, the greater the likelihood that we will relegate certain children to lower levels of expectation and academic opportunity (Green et al., 2005). For example, an African American chemist working for a Fortune 500 company told me recently that he and his wife had to advocate every year for their two sons *not* to be placed in special education classes. In this small-town community, where their sons were among very few children of color, teachers would routinely refer these two boys to remedial classrooms. Strangely enough, this occurred in spite of the fact that both students performed well in regular and even advanced classes.

Eventually, each of these young men went on to graduate from prestigious colleges and acquire lucrative positions, which leads me to wonder what would have happened to them without the advantage of parents who could resist the assumptions of school personnel. Rigid, unexamined, and unchallenged assumptions about children of color on the part of White educators are one of the important factors contributing to the overrepresentation of Black, Hispanic, and Native American children in segregated special education classrooms in our nation's schools (Boyd & Correa, 2005; Fierros & Conroy, 2001; Green et al., 2005; Hebbeler et al., 2001).

For the vast majority of educators who, like me, grew up in predominantly White suburban communities, it is logical to assume that the culture and practice of schooling, as presently constituted, work well for all students. From our assumption of rightness, we can easily conclude that our professional judgments are correct and that those who don't achieve, or don't perform in ways that are comfortable and familiar to us, are either not sufficiently intelligent or inadequately supported by their home environment. The deficiency, from this point of view, lies in the child or in the home, and not in the system of schooling or in the shortcomings of educators. Transformationist White teachers reject these facile assumptions and take responsibility for unraveling the classroom inequities that have perpetuated the achievement gap.

The luxury of ignorance allows many dominant culture educators to remain unaware of the intense "socio-cultural misalignment between home and school" (Comer, 1988, p. 44) that is experienced by students from poor and racially diverse backgrounds. Even for those children of color who are successful, school is often experienced as a foreign environment (Aronson, 2004; Steele, 2004). An African American athlete attending a predominantly White high school described his experience this way to one of my colleagues: "I'm doing OK in school, but it's just that every day seems like an away game" (Diane Turner, personal communication, 2003). On the other hand, for me and for most of my White middle-class colleagues, the neighborhood school in the suburbs was a direct reflection of our home environment. For us, every day was a home game. We enjoyed the easy comfort of a smooth transition between home and school, and have assumed that ought to be true for the diverse children we now teach (Darder, 1991, 2002; Lawrence-Lightfoot, 2003).

One of the dilemmas of White dominance is that we are often blind to the negative impact that our imagined goodness and narrow sense of normalcy have on others who do not share the demographic advantages that have favored our group. We see ourselves as doing good work by serving "those kids," often without connecting emotionally and personally with our students' actual lived experiences (Delpit, 1996, 2002). Transformationist White educators have the courage to challenge our own luxury of ignorance. We choose to enter into the worldview of our students and their families; we choose to know that which our privilege has allowed us not to know. Thus, we choose consciousness over dysconsciousness and in the process become advocates for change.

The legacy of privilege refers to those advantages, like school success, that flow to some and not to others, based solely on membership in the dominant group. The function of privilege is illustrated in a story told by an Hispanic high school student entering her first day in an honors AP English classroom. She was the only student of color in the class, and the teacher pulled her aside at the end of the session to ask, "Are you sure you want to be in here? This is going to be a very challenging course." The teacher's insensitivity merely exacerbated this young woman's already heightened sense of aloneness and otherness in the AP classroom. The privilege comes in the fact that none of the Anglo students were asked that same question.

Privilege is also exercised in the many strategies employed by families, politicians, and even educators who seek to escape or abandon public education in communities that are urban, poor, and predominantly populated by children of color. For decades we have witnessed White flight to the suburbs, and "good schools" have in many people's minds become synonymous with "White schools." Today we see a more complex phenomenon, wherein families from all racial and ethnic backgrounds, once they have achieved a level of economic success, will follow the money to the suburbs or to private schools, thus creating a kind of green flight that continues to drain valuable human and economic resources from our core cities and most challenged environments. Another manifestation of privilege is the movement toward voucher programs that may serve some students well, but will eventually exacerbate the concentration of poverty and failure in urban schools while creating enclaves of elitism for a privileged few (Cookson, 1991).

I present this discussion of social dominance not for the purpose of casting blame, but with the hope of increasing our clarity and consciousness regarding the deeper dynamics underlying the achievement gap and the real issues of school reform. Because transformationist White teachers understand how schooling has been shaped by the forces of social dominance, we are less likely to impose our narrow cultural lens on the experiences of those who have not benefited from these dynamics of privilege and favored position. By acknowledging that racial and socioeconomic inequities and the resulting achievement gap are a logical consequence of our system of education, and not an aberration, we as transformationist White educators are more likely to work for personal, professional, and institutional growth rather than casting aspersions on the idiosyncratic failures of students, parents, or their racial-cultural communities. In reality, we are all socialized into systems of dominance that are highly resistant to change; therefore, it is both ourselves and the systems of dominance that must be transformed.

An essential part of educational reform and eliminating the achievement gap is the work of unraveling social dominance. This is the challenge that focuses the energy and imagination of transformationist White educators and informs both what we *know* and what we *do* in our classroom practice.

WHAT TRANSFORMATIONIST TEACHERS KNOW

An African American principal in an urban elementary school recently asked me to provide a workshop for her predominantly White female faculty. Her teachers were complaining about "behavior problems" with their African American male students, and the principal thought that by inviting me, a White educator, to talk about the issue, perhaps her teachers would be less resistant than they had been in her repeated efforts to address the situation.

Since this was an urban school, with an experienced staff and 80% of the students being children of color, I assumed the faculty would be receptive to an open conversation about race. I began the session by saying, "Since most of you are White women and most of your perceived discipline problems are with Black males, let's begin by talking about issues of race and gender and how these issues may be influencing your interactions with your students." This approach did not work.

The principal and the three faculty members of color were more than willing to deal with issues of race, but the vast majority of the White teachers were uncomfortable and resistant to this line of engagement. My mere mention of "stages of White identity development" produced an angry reaction from several teachers who told me that they did not identify as "White." I suggested in response, "Even though you may not choose this racial descriptor for yourselves, your Black male students definitely see you as White, and perhaps we should try to understand these issues through their eyes." This produced an even more hostile reaction, and it was clear to me that I had not entered this work in the most helpful way for this particular school.

Race Matters

I use this story to illustrate one of the most basic things that transformationist White teachers know; namely, that race is a central factor in our interaction with our students of color. I know that the first thing my students of color notice about me is that I am White. No matter how I may try to dance around the issue, my Whiteness is real to them. Whatever their past experiences and perceptions of White people may have been, that is how they will initially experience me. Ultimately, neither we nor our students have to be controlled by these perceptions; however, as White teachers we must know that race is real (Applebaum, 2000; Johnson, 2001; Ladson-Billings, 2002; Tatum, 2003). Cornel West (1993b) is right; the race card is always at play. How teachers deal with it is what makes the difference in the lives of our students.

If I am having disproportionate discipline problems with my students of color, a possible racial/cultural disconnection is the first thing I need to consider. The teachers I described above, by refusing to acknowledge their own Whiteness as a possible factor in their relationships with Black male students, were merely exacerbating the problem. As one of these teachers declared, "I teach a color-blind curriculum, so race is not a factor in my classroom." When we fail to recognize the racialized nature of our identity as White people, we are ignoring the potential for race-based barriers between ourselves and our students and thereby contributing to the reproduction of racial inequalities in our nation's schools (A. Ferguson, 2000; Lewis, 2003). To be worthy of our students, we as transformationist White teachers know that we must be intelligent and real about issues of race.

Change Begins With Us

In addition to our knowledge and competence in dealing with issues of race, transformationist teachers also know that educational equity and school reform, in large part, depend on White educators' willingness to engage in the process of our own personal and professional growth. Since we comprise the vast majority of the nation's teachers, school transformation is largely about changing us, our classroom practices, and the structures of schooling that have been built on a foundation of White dominance. What most bothered the teachers in the above anecdote was my suggestion that the solution to their "discipline problems" may, in fact, have more to do with their own growth and development rather than with any perceived behavioral deficiencies they were projecting onto their Black male students.

In contrast to this situation, I have worked for 3 years in another urban school district with a similar student population, where teachers and administrators (mostly White) have committed themselves to an ongoing and in-depth exploration of their own attitudes, beliefs, and practices related to race and cultural differences. These educators have publicly acknowledged that they cannot reasonably approach issues of the achievement gap without significantly enhancing their own awareness and effectiveness in cross-racial and cross-cultural interactions. Transformationist White educators know that if we don't grow in this way, nothing else will significantly shift (Cochran-Smith, Davis, & Fries, 2004; Howard, 2002).

Beliefs Determine Outcomes

A Native American colleague, Roger Fernandes, often begins his teacher workshops with two rhetorical questions: "Is it possible for a teacher to make students believe that the teacher believes in them?" And conversely, "Is it possible for a teacher to make students believe that the teacher does not believe in them?" The answers, of course, are affirmative in both cases, but the questions themselves invite a deeper conversation about the ways in which teacher expectations and beliefs about our students determine their performance in our classrooms. Transformationist White educators know that our beliefs are a powerful determinant of our students' achievement.

For many students of color, success in school is like being invited to a party for which the location and date remain unannounced. Even if they wanted to go, how would they get there? Indeed, in one of the school districts where I have been involved over the past few years, the superintendent interviewed academically talented high school students of color and asked them why they were not enrolled in higher level courses such as honors and advanced placement. These were students who could work at the higher levels, but were not engaged there. Their answers clustered in three ways: (1) I don't want to be alone, (2) I didn't know that I could, and (3) I don't want to fail. I find these data to be a tragic embodiment of the dominance paradigm, wherein talented students of color do not even see the possibility of their own success at higher levels in the educational system. And even if they do see this possibility, their capacity to risk and their sense of confidence are often limited by the "stereotype threat" that burdens the performance of many students of color (Aronson & Steele, 2005; Steele, 2004). A sense of belonging and a feeling of trust in the social setting are key variables that can diminish the negative impact of stereotype threat (Aronson, 2004); thus our clear communication of belief in our students is a critical factor in freeing them to connect with their own intelligence (Rosenthal, 2002; Weinstein, 2002). In the absence of adults who can effectively and passionately communicate their belief in the possibility of excellence, even high-ability students of color will continue to languish in mediocrity, and thus we perpetuate a process whereby higher level courses are allowed to remain essentially White enclaves of exclusivity.

Transformationist White educators know that school reality does not have to be this way. Encouraged by the Education Trust's identification of 4,000 high-performing, high-diversity, high-poverty schools (Education Trust, 2002; Noguera, 2003), we are strengthened in our knowledge that the problem lies not in the students themselves, but in our capacity to believe in them. One of these belief-driven schools is Hawthorne Elementary, located in Seattle's most racially diverse and lowest income neighborhood. When my colleague John Morefield became principal of Hawthorne in the 1980s, he staked his job on turning around the school's low achievement history, promising that all entering kindergarten children would graduate from fifth grade with skills at or above grade level proficiency. He transformed the staff by hiring only those teachers who demonstrated high belief in their students' ability to learn, and working together over the years they delivered on the promise. At a recent high school graduation awards assembly, where many former Hawthorne students received academic honors for their exceptional performance in higher level courses, John was told by several students after the ceremony that "You and our teachers at Hawthorne made us believe that we were smarter than we thought we were."

Transformationist educators, like John Morefield and the Hawthorne staff, know that authentic school reform is about much more than merely raising standards. Mandating higher standards and expectations, without a concomitant belief in our students' capacity to meet and exceed those standards, only leads to frustration, failure, and a promise denied (Darling-Hammond, 2004). On the other hand, high expectations that are seamlessly linked to a deep and persistent commitment to the power of belief in our students' intelligence can provide the only real foundation for school change.

Teaching Is a Calling, Not Just a Job

Parker Palmer reminds us that "true vocation joins self and service" (2000, p. 16). He points out that the deeper meaning of "vocation," which derives from the Latin for "voice," literally means that our true work is more a *calling* we hear rather than merely a *job* that we do (p. 4). With the data showing that teachers in racially diverse and low-income schools have the highest absenteeism and turnover rates of any teachers in the country (Barton, 2004), it is especially important for transformationist White teachers to see our vocation as our life's work, imbued with deep meaning for both ourselves and our students.

Timothy Bunch is a nationally recognized educator who teaches in a juvenile justice detention center in South Carolina. He is a White teacher who has been working primarily with African American males for over a decade, and he says of his work:

> I believe I am called to teach, from a spiritual standpoint as well as a professional standpoint. I think like a teacher; everything is a lesson. I want kids to love learning as much as I do. (*USA Today*, March 21, 2005, p. 6D)

Teachers who think like Timothy Bunch will choose to work in even the most challenging school settings precisely because they know it is their calling (Nieto, 2005b). John Morefield, in his reflections on the Hawthorne success story, writes about the choice to teach in diverse schools:

> Deciding to go into teaching must be a decision from the heart. It must come from a moral imperative to ensure the success of all children, and from a deeply held commitment to social justice. . . . Our children cannot afford anything but the best from us. (1996, p. 9)

Transformationist White teachers know that our work is a life-long journey in the service of a larger vision, a relentless and passionate quest to undo the tragic impact of White dominance, and thereby free our children to enjoy the full fruits of their own intelligence and success.

THE ACHIEVEMENT TRIANGLE

The process of growth toward transformationist White identity requires the acquisition of many new ways of knowing. For those of us who choose to teach in racially diverse schools, this knowing comprises at least the four arenas mentioned above: that race matters, that change begins with us, that beliefs greatly influence outcomes, and that teaching is a calling, not just a job. In my workshops with teachers throughout the country, I have found it helpful to provide a visual representation—the Achievement Triangle—that summarizes the dimensions of knowing that are necessary for us to be effective in our work for educational equity (see Figure 7.1).

The base of the Achievement Triangle represents **"knowing my prac-tice."** Research shows that children of color and children in poverty are disproportionately exposed to teachers who are underqualified and un-derprepared (Barton, 2004; Darling-Hammond, 2004), so it is essential that we, as transformationist White teachers, know our practice well (Elmore, 2002; Resnick & Harwell, 1998). This entails a highly complex set of pro-fessional knowledge, including curriculum, pedagogy, instructional de-sign, developmental psychology, history and philosophy of education,

Figure 7.1.   Achievement Triangle: Dimensions of Knowing

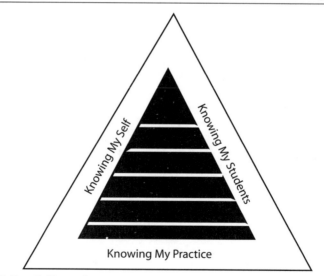

Knowing My Self

Knowing My Students

Knowing My Practice

legal issues, human relations, cross-cultural communication, conflict management, and more. It is difficult to imagine a profession that requires a broader foundation of essential knowledge. Much of what we need to know in these many arenas is transmitted through our teacher preparation programs, but we must acquire even more on the job, when we are finally forced to step outside the comfort zone of our constructed reality. This dimension of the Achievement Triangle, in itself, requires a lifetime of study, yet at best it represents only a third of what we must know to be effective in diverse classrooms.

The second dimension of knowing represented by the Achievement Triangle relates to the complex set of experiences that lead to **"knowing my self."** Sadly, this is an arena of knowledge for which we receive little time, attention, or encouragement in most teacher preparation programs. However, as we saw in our discussion of White racial identity development in Chapters 5 and 6, as well as in the "Change Begins with Us" section above, self-knowledge is perhaps one of the most critical factors in determining our effectiveness as White teachers in multiracial schools. The more I have examined my own "stuff" related to race, culture, and difference, the less likely it is that I will consciously or unconsciously expose students to my own assumption of rightness, my luxury of ignorance, or my blind perpetuation of the legacy of White privilege. As Parker Palmer (1988) reminds us, "We teach who we are" (p. 1). An unexamined life on the part of a White teacher is a danger to every student.

The third dimension of the Achievement Triangle engages the teacher in **"knowing my students."** Like the other two sides of the triangle, this arena also calls for a complex kind of knowing, one that relates to the cultures, racial identities, languages, family backgrounds, home situations, learning characteristics, economic status, personalities, strengths and challenges, and uniqueness of each of our students. Similar to knowing my practice and knowing my self, this is an arena of knowledge for which we can never reach full capacity. Yet, the extent to which we *can* know who our students really are is the extent to which we can avoid projecting onto them our own imagined assumptions and biases (Darder, 1991, 2002; Freire, 2004; Hale, 2004). The more we can know our students, the more we can authentically engage them in the learning process.

Knowing our practice, knowing our selves, knowing our students—these are the essential elements of knowledge that keep good teachers engaged and effective in our classrooms (Nieto, 2003, 2005b). These are arenas of knowing that allow us to do our work as transformationist White teachers. And it is to this "doing" that we now turn our attention.

WHAT TRANSFORMATIONIST TEACHERS DO

By focusing on the points of intersection that connect the three sides of the Achievement Triangle, we can highlight the dimensions of action that are the necessary work of transformationist White teachers. Each of these points of intersection functions as a doorway connecting what we *know* about our practice with what we *do* in the service of our students (see Figure 7.2).

The Doorway of Rigor

For the transformationist White teacher, "knowing my self" means having a deep sense of my identity as a White person, acknowledging that race matters in my life, and holding a passionate commitment to confront and unravel issues of dominance in my own experience. When this deep sense of "knowing my self" intersects with "knowing my practice," my approach to teaching is energized in ways that would never have happened had I

Figure 7.2. Achievement Triangle: Dimensions of Action

Copyright © Gary R. Howard

not chosen to become conscious of the realities of race, Whiteness, and social dominance. From this intersection of self and practice, we develop a life-long commitment to personal growth and a passion for equity in our professional life. From this passion grows our commitment to be focused and rigorous in our work, not rigor for its own sake, but a seriousness about our practice that is energized by our deep desire to overturn the effects of injustice and dominance in the lives of our students.

In sharp contrast to this stance, a White urban high school teacher said in a workshop I was conducting for his faculty: "I'm getting along well with my students of color and, frankly, I don't think I have any more need for personal transformation." He said this in spite of the fact that students of color in his school, as a group, were performing far below proficiency in his teaching area of mathematics. A White teacher who is not rigorously engaged in an ongoing process of growth, both as a person and as a professional, is a threat to the well-being and success of all students.

Transformationist White teachers are always in the process of personal and professional transformation. We are serious about our work; we are rigorous in our practice; we are continually assessing our own effectiveness. We are forever fighting not to reinforce the substantial data that show White teachers in urban diverse schools to be underqualified and poorly prepared to teach students of color (Gomez, 1996; Grossman, Beaupre, & Rossi, 2001; Haycock, 2004; Zeichner, 1996a, 1996b). Rigor means being relentless in our belief in our students capacity to learn, and being equally vigilant in improving our capacity to teach. It means caring deeply about our students and about our practice. It means having a passion for equity and social justice.

The Doorway of Relationship

The second doorway of action related to the Achievement Triangle is opened where "knowing my self" meets "knowing my students." The degree to which I know myself as a racial being is the extent to which I can enter into authentic relationships with my students of color. The process of self-awareness and growth toward authentic White racial identity is important precisely because it enables us to relate more effectively across differences in race. As Geneva Gay (2000) reminds us, "The personal is powerful" (p. 198).

It is important to clarify here what we mean by "relationships" with our students. We are not talking about being best friends or buddies with our students. Neither are we talking about a soft-hearted do-gooder approach or a missionary stance of "helping the less fortunate" (Ladson-Billings, 2001, p. 17). An authentic professional relationship is one that communicates clearly to my students through my words, my actions, and my attitudes the following sense of connection: "I see you. I acknowledge your presence in this classroom. I know your name and I can pronounce it correctly. I respect your life experiences and your intelligence. I believe in you and I will hold both you and myself accountable to honor your capacity to learn. I enjoy being in this work with you." Good teachers have always approached their students in this way. Many years ago Judith Kleinfeld (1975) found that this strong sense of focus, respect, and "warm demand" on the part of teachers was the key to working successfully with Native Alaskan children (see also Vasquez, 1988).

Another way to approach the doorway of relationship is through the concept of cultural competence. I define cultural competence as the *will* and the *ability* to form authentic and effective relationships across difference. Thus, cultural competence is about *choice* and it is about *skill*. Transformationist White teachers choose to pay attention to issues of race and other differences in our relationships with our students, and we continually grow in our ability to relate effectively with them. "Authentic" in this definition of cultural competence means that our students trust that we are being real. Students have antennae for authenticity, and they know whether we are being genuine with them. "Effective" in the definition means that the relationships are working, that our students across their many differences are learning, that the doorway to the house of success is being opened to them.

Obviously, not all students need a personal relationship with us in order to succeed in school. We all know students who can learn without us, and sometimes even in spite of us. But for those students who have been most burdened by the history of social dominance and are, therefore, caught in the lower realms of the achievement gap, an authentic relationship with us often necessarily precedes their learning (Maslow, 1962; Shade, Kelly, & Oberg, 1997). Without knowing us and being authentically known by us, they simply will not succeed. This is why White teachers who have not seriously engaged the journey toward cultural competence and authentic White identity cannot teach effectively in racially diverse schools. To be worthy of our students and to be effective with them, transformationist White teachers are persistent and passionate in our efforts to create personal connections that work.

The Doorway of Responsiveness

The third point of intersection on the Achievement Triangle is the place where the "self" of the student meets the "stuff" of our teaching. This is the rubber-hits-the-road dimension where our students connect with the curriculum through our pedagogy. This is the place where the first grader learns to read, where the middle school student masters algebra, and where the high school junior acquires the capacity to write a powerful expository essay.

"Responsiveness" has to do with our capacity as teachers to know and connect with the actual lived experience, personhood, and learning modalities of the students who are in our classroom. It is amazing to me in my travels to schools throughout the country how many educators want to imagine that their students are somebody other than who they really are. In one such place, a high school teacher stood in an audience of 500 of her colleagues and lamented the fact that "I'm using the same teaching strategies that have been successful for me for the past 25 years, and somehow these students today just don't want to work." This occurred in a school district outside New York City that had experienced a rapid demographic shift over the past decade, transitioning from a student population that was primarily White and wealthy to one that is now (through White-flight and green-flight) 85% students of color and 60% low-income. The young people this teacher referred to as "these students today" represent a rich mixture of Haitian, Jamaican, Dominican, African American, Hispanic, and European American backgrounds. In response to her remark, I said to her and the gathered audience, "Thank you for your comment. It points out something that is true for many teachers in school districts like yours that have experienced rapid change in student population. Many of us are doing a great job of teaching the kids who *used* to live here, but who simply aren't in our classrooms anymore. What we need to learn to do now is teach the kids who *are* here."

Learning to teach the students who are actually in our classrooms is referred to in the literature as "culturally relevant" or "culturally responsive" teaching. Ladson-Billings (1994) identifies three essential arenas of this work: (1) concept of self and others, (2) structure of interactions, and (3) construction of knowledge. Thus, reinforcing our above discussion of the Achievement Triangle, Ladson-Billings challenges educators in diverse classrooms to know who we are and to know our students well, to be competent in the structuring of relationships that work, and to allow space for the students' authentic cultural knowledge to inform and intersect creatively with our teaching.

From another point of view, Shade, Kelly, and Oberg (1997) offer seven principles for building culturally responsive learning communities: (1) affirming students in their cultural connections, (2) being personally inviting, (3) creating physically welcoming classroom spaces, (4) reinforcing students for their academic development, (5) accommodating our instruction to the cultural and learning style differences of our students, (6) managing our classrooms with firm, consistent, and loving control, and (7) creating opportunities for both individual and cooperative work. A third perspective is provided by Gay (2000), who examines culturally responsive teaching under four arenas of teacher behavior: (1) caring, (2) communication, (3) curriculum, and (4) instruction. A fourth researcher,

McKinley (2005), has spent countless hours observing culturally responsive teachers who have demonstrated their effectiveness in working with African American students, and from these observations has isolated key strategies that work. One of the factors that she found to be most effective is the willingness and ability of the teacher to employ a constructivist approach that utilizes the students' personal and cultural knowledge as the basis of inquiry in the classroom. Thus, through our responsiveness to the "funds-of-knowledge" that students carry with them into the classroom, we are able to tap into greater reservoirs of engagement and intellect (Moll & González, 2004).

Whichever theoretical approach we take, the work of culturally responsive teaching calls us to a deep engagement with each of the elements we have explored through the lens of the Achievement Triangle. The work of transformationist teachers is to know our practice well. The more diverse our students are, the more serious we must be in our beliefs and expectations for them, and the more rigorous we must be in continually improving our pedagogy. We must also know ourselves well and have significantly engaged the journey toward authentic racial identity, so that we are culturally competent and capable of forming authentic relationships with our students. Likewise, we must know our students well, both for the purpose of building relationships that work, and also for the purpose of designing curriculum and pedagogical strategies that are responsive to, and honoring of, our students' actual lived experiences. There is no work more complex, and there is no work more important, than this.

TOWARD A TRANSFORMATIONIST PEDAGOGY

In this book we have primarily and intentionally engaged issues of race, dominance, social justice, and educational reform from the perspective of White teachers. Whereas it is essential that White educators grow in the ways discussed here, it must also be acknowledged that transformationist teaching is a challenge and a necessity for all educators, whatever our racial or cultural identities may be.

Following a presentation in Kentucky, an African American graduate student stayed after my session to continue the discussion of culturally responsive teaching that I had facilitated. She told me a story about her own teaching that illuminates the need for all of us to grow in this work. Having attended public school in a predominantly White school district and then college at a primarily White university, where she studied to be a foreign language teacher, she described herself as "educated to be White." Her first teaching job was in a White suburban community, and there she experienced a high level of success in teaching high school French. Her next teaching assignment was in a predominantly Black community, where she was utterly frustrated and unsuccessful and "went home crying every night." She said, "The kids were totally disengaged, and I finally realized that the way I had learned French and the way I had been taught to teach it were all from a White frame of reference. Even though I was racially identified with my Black students, I was totally out of touch with them in terms of my approach to teaching." In her efforts to adjust to this challenge, she "had to walk myself around all three sides of the Achievement Triangle—getting to know myself better, to understand where the students were coming from, and the main thing was to work on the quality of my relationships with them before I could engage more effectively in the teaching." Her story graphically illustrates that knowing ourselves, forming authentic relationships with our students, and teaching through culturally responsive strategies are difficult and necessary challenges for all educators, regardless of whether we are race-alike or race-different from our students.

Teaching from a transformationist perspective requires all educators to step out of the dominance programming that is so pervasive throughout our educational institutions and to discover an alternative and more authentic way to engage both across and within our various ethnic and racial communities. Transformationist pedagogy is the place where our **passion for equity** intersects with our **cultural competence** and leads to **culturally responsive teaching** in our classrooms and schools (see Figure 7.3).

Transformationist pedagogy means teaching and leading in such a way that more of our students, across more of their differences, achieve at a higher level, more of the time, without giving up who they are. In the transformationist classroom the price of success is not assimilation ("acting White"), but rather a process of deep engagement with authentic identity and one's own intellectual efficacy. The reward in such classrooms is that everyone gets smarter together, including the teacher, while at the same time maintaining, strengthening, and honoring our differences.

In the presence of our students we are called to be gracious, competent, courageous, and worthy. If we offer ourselves in this way, we earn the right to expect from our students their respect, engagement, honesty, and effort. The doors of responsiveness must swing both ways, yet we know, as a function of our professionalism, that the greater burden is, and ought to be, on us. In this light, the urban high school teacher who said in one of my workshops, "I teach and the kids decide whether to learn," is both a danger and a disgrace to our profession.

Figure 7.3. Achievement Triangle: Transformationist Pedagogy

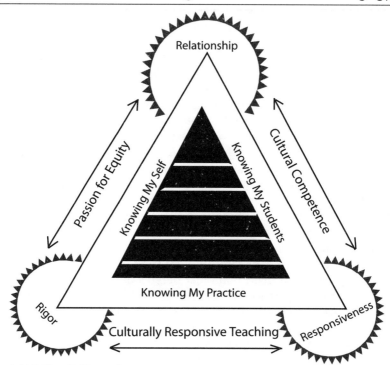

THE POLITICS OF GOOD TEACHING

In addition to what we know and what we do in our transformationist practice, it is also important to acknowledge that any realistic attempts to deal with issues of educational equity and school reform necessarily push us to broaden our frame of reference beyond teachers and the schools. From a larger perspective, we cannot eliminate the achievement gap and attain greater educational excellence simply by looking for solutions and strategies solely *within* the educational system (Anyon, 1997). As Albert Einstein reminded us from his own creative work, we cannot solve a problem from the same level of thinking we were at when we created the problem.

Beyond issues of pedagogy and classroom practice, one of the core problem that challenges us within public education is the same one we face as a nation in our current political and economic climate. One of the central problems of our time is that we, as a nation, have drifted too far toward proliferating the greed and power of the few and too far away from protecting and empowering the good of the many. A strong national commitment to public education is the quintessential embodiment of "the public good." This sacred trust to protect the good of the many is at the heart of our struggle for educational equity; it is the nesting ground for school reform, and it is the place from which we can best birth and nurture our shared national future as a free and democratic people.

The forces of social dominance, as we have seen in our previous discussion, are, by definition, directed toward protecting and perpetuating the good of the few. Whether this be in the form of school privatization schemes that divert public education dollars into for-profit enterprises that will serve only a fraction of our most needy students, or voucher proposals that would put public resources into private hands, or national mandates that threaten to take already-inadequate levels of funding away from our nation's most challenged schools and communities, or massive tax breaks for the rich that drive our nation into such a state of economic deficit that we cannot even entertain a meaningful discussion of adequate educational funding. The mentality underlying these policies and proposals is clearly not in the best interests of "the many."

For this reason and in this context, public school educators are, by the nature of our work, political operatives. I speak here not of partisan politics in the traditional sense of Democrats versus Republicans. Rather I invoke the deeper meaning of politics in terms of passionate commitment to serve the people well. All evidence to date shows that neither political party has the courage, the vision, or the will to take on the real issues of social inequality that underpin the achievement gap. Rather than the current politics of abandonment we need a new politics of engagement that is dedicated to the recovery of democracy, the renewal of a vital public education system, and the preservation of our children's future (West, 2004).

In our role as educators we are either acting in complicity with the forces of dominance that underlie the achievement gap, or we are consciously and actively seeking to subvert these dynamics and inequities in the service of our students (Tatum, 2003). When it comes to issues of social justice and educational equity, it is difficult or impossible to find a middle ground. We are either being used by the forces of dominance, or we are actively resisting them, both in our personhood and in our professional practice. Whether we are in complicity or in resistance, we have tremendous political influence.

Part of the work of transformationist educators of all racial and cultural groups is to make known that which the forces of dominance would prefer us to leave unnamed and unacknowledged, namely, that (1) the political climate in which public education is currently embedded is not working for the children who have already been pushed to the margins by the equities inherent in systems of social dominance (McNeil, 2000), that (2) those who benefit from these systems have no real intention to change the dynamics that have historically favored them, and that (3) much of the rhetoric underlying the lofty claims of "no child left behind" is merely window-dressing and dramatic illusion on the stage of perpetual dominance (Comer, 2004; Meier & Wood, 2005; Sleeter, 2006). As Dr. John Mackiel, superintendent of the Omaha Public Schools, said recently in an address to his principals and leadership team, "Most of what we are being asked to do to comply with current federal mandates is simply not in the best interest of our students" (personal communication, March 22, 2005).

In addition to what we know and do in our schools, transformationist teachers are passionate and vigilant in our efforts to expand the arena of our own personal and political consciousness, to unravel the roots of dominance that continue to stifle achievement in our classrooms, and to create schools that are worthy of our students and compatible with the highest values of pluralistic democracy. We are relentless in our passion to serve the good of the many over the greed of the few. We, as transformationist teachers, are "the primary stewards of democracy" (Parker, 2003, p. xvii). Reflecting back on the Irish poet's words that opened this chapter, this is "the new idea" that "cannot be returned or reversed" (O'Donohue, 2004, p. 43). This is our vision; this is our unfinished work.

CHAPTER 8

Our Unfinished Work: White Educators and *La Tierra Transformativa*

> With malice toward none; with charity for all; with firmness in the right, as God gives us to see the right, let us strive on to finish the work we are in; to bind up the nation's wounds . . . and to do all which may achieve and cherish a just and lasting peace among ourselves and with all nations.
> —Abraham Lincoln, Second Inaugural Address

My home in the foothills of the Cascade Mountains is located at the end of a long private road overarched with cedar, fir, and alder trees. It is a rustic and bumpy path, damaged yearly by the ubiquitous northwest rains and occasional winter frosts. Where the blacktop ends and our road begins, the county has posted a sign: "Primitive Road. No Warning Signs. Proceed with Caution." On the official maps at the county courthouse our road is drawn in dotted lines with a notation: "Location of road uncertain." Given its rough, unmarked, and unmapped character, our country road reminds me of the journey toward authentic and positive White identity, a journey that is also difficult to define and has been similarly subjected to the erosive damage of time.

COMPLEXITY AND CHOICE

Whiteness is at best a dissonant identity. To be aware of one's Whiteness is to be in conflict, at least to some degree, with the social marker of race that we carry. Whiteness has been associated for centuries with racism and dominance. It is an inescapable truth of history that Whites are inherently implicated in the legacy of privilege and have benefited from the oppression of other groups. In my own family, for example, our ancestors over several generations in America have been farmers and railroad workers, both endeavors dependent on vast amounts of land taken from Native people.

Yet this oppressive past is only part of the picture of White identity. As discussed in Chapter 6, it is a mistake to assume that White racial identity is synonymous with oppression. Whereas the weight of dominance is part of our collective baggage, it is also true that many White educators and activists have dedicated our personal and professional lives to the work of equity and social transformation. We have sought both to transform ourselves and to engage our White students and colleagues in the search for an authentic White identity based on a desire for justice rather than a dependence on dominance.

Our discussion throughout this book has clearly demonstrated that White racial identity is a multidimensional and complex phenomenon. Ours is a "multiple, shifting, and often contradictory identity" (Wall, 1989, p. 10). We are both racist and antiracist, both part of the problem and part of the solution, both benefiting from oppression as well as opposing it. The complex and conflicted nature of White racial identity is consistent with Stuart Hall's notion of "the new ethnicity" (cited in Giroux, 1997b, p. 298). From Hall's (1996) perspective, Whiteness becomes "a politically and culturally constructed category" that is dynamic and always shifting, never fixed or finalized (p. 443). Theories of White racial identity and the model of White identity orientations presented here are clear evidence that there is not one way of being White, but many.

Whiteness is a multidimensional and often ambiguous descriptor, causing considerable confusion for those of us who are seeking to establish some clarity in our own identity. As Whites we are not alone in this experience of complexity for, as Salman Rushdie (1997) says of his own search for identity in the multicultural nation of India,

> In the modern age, we have come to understand our own selves as composites, often contradictory, even internally incompatible. We have understood that each of us is many different people. . . . The 19th century concept of the integrated self has been replaced by this jostling crowd of "I"s. (p. 42)

Given the complexity and internal tension related to Whiteness, there is a sense of marginality about White identity that casts a tentative and illusory shadow over any positive images we might achieve. As Griffin (1995) writes of her attempts to fashion a secure sense of identity as a White woman, "It has taken me a long time to see my wavering ambivalence as other than a character flaw—to begin to see the margin as tenable, a valid position in many cases, even a place of vision" (p. 9). Exploring the uncertain margins of her racial identity, she draws inspiration from Tillich (1966):

> I thought that the concept of the boundary might be the fitting symbol for the whole of my personal and intellectual development. At almost every point, I have had to stand between alternate possibilities of existence, to be completely at home in neither and to take no definitive stand. Since thinking presupposes receptiveness to new possibilities, this position is fruitful for thought; but it is difficult and dangerous for life. (p. 13)

White identity exists in the margins. We are like a people caught between two lands. There is the old country of oppression and racism from which we are attempting to emigrate, and the new country of hope, transformation, and healing that we are now beginning to explore and inhabit. We have of necessity been border travelers, attempting to map a new route toward positive White identity, while at the same time being inextricably tied to the weight of former images.

The road to a transformationist White orientation is neither straight nor easy. It is neither well mapped nor well traveled. It is a journey fraught with ambiguity, complexity, and dissonance. Our travels do not take us further away from Whiteness but continually engage us more deeply with it. We can never fully free ourselves from the oppressive elements of Whiteness because the dominance paradigm continues to enmesh us in the legacy of privilege. In this sense there is no purity to be found in Whiteness. There is no alternative route that will allow us to dissolve our identity. Those who claim to have discovered such a pathway *out* of Whiteness merely demonstrate their limited awareness of the depth and complexity of our journey.

There is, however, a sense of excitement and an invigorating challenge to be found on the road to an emergent transformationist White identity. There is a feeling of adventure and discovery in growing toward greater awareness. There is personal renewal and hope to be found in the possibility of change and the opportunity to believe and act in new ways. There is a positive and healing privilege gained through our connection and collaboration with colleagues and students from other racial, ethnic, and cultural groups. And there is joy in knowing that we have chosen to be in this struggle, that we are part of a movement to dismantle the foundation of our own past and present dominance. The reward for transformative White educators is that we have a vision worthy of a lifetime of work.

COMMUNITY AND CHANGE

As White educators we have a unique opportunity to help shift the tide of racial dominance. Although we have inextricably benefited from our position as Whites in Western nations, we now have a choice to turn the full force of our privilege and power toward dismantling the very system that has granted us our historical advantage. Because we represent such a large majority of the teacher population today, we can have tremendous influence in determining the course of educational change. Before we can effectively engage in this transformational work, however, there is much we need to learn about the nature and dynamics of dominance. As we have seen in the previous chapters, there is also much that White educators must *unlearn* regarding our assumptions of rightness and the easy ignorance that has comforted Whites for generations in our position of social hegemony. For those of us who choose to work on issues of racial healing, there is a complex and difficult path leading to cultural competence and the development of transformationist identity and pedagogy.

It is important to acknowledge that White educators cannot travel alone on the road to authenticity and social healing. As was made clear in my own story, and from the many voices of White educators cited throughout this text, each of us who has embarked on the journey toward transformationist White identity has been mentored along the way by teachers, colleagues, students, friends, relatives, or lovers from other racial and cultural groups. Cross-border connections have been the catalysts for our growth. Each of us has been given the gift of relationship with someone who provided the lens whereby we came to view our Whiteness from the outside, someone who helped us become self-reflective regarding our own racial identity. It has been neither their obligation nor their responsibility to guide us in this way, but a blessing for us when they have chosen to do so.

In 1976, when I first began my work in multicultural education and was teaching in a 98% White rural school district, I often felt like a lone voice in a sea of Whiteness. For my own personal and professional survival, I sought the advice and counsel of colleagues of color working in local universities and metropolitan areas. Some were justifiably skeptical of me as a White male trying to bring multicultural awareness to predominantly White schools, but most were generously supportive in offering their time, resources, and expertise. Many of these colleagues later came to my school district to share their perspectives and knowledge with teachers and students. Several helped author and review the REACH multicultural materials. Some became close friends or members of the REACH board of directors, and a few later joined our staff.

I could not have survived the early years of my work in this field without these friends and allies from other racial and cultural groups. From them I learned that Whites alone cannot accomplish the work of social healing and transformation. If we are to be effective and sustained in our efforts, White educators must be immersed in a co-responsible community of support with a richly diverse group of peers, mentors, and allies. I also learned from my experiences that the vision of equity and social justice cannot be achieved solely through the work of our colleagues of color. They need our support as much as we need theirs, particularly in relation to changing the attitudes of White people and dismantling the dominance paradigm in schools and other social institutions.

For the past 30 years I have been blessed to be part of a close multi-cultural network of colleagues and friends, the REACH national trainer network, which includes educators from a wide variety of racial, religious, ethnic, and cultural groups throughout the United States and Australia. We work together in diverse teams of two or three trainers at a time, attempting to bring a transformative multicultural vision to teachers, administrators, students, and community leaders in a wide variety of settings, often working within the context of highly charged and resistant environments. Over the years, many close personal relationships have evolved from this collegial network. We meet annually to nurture our friendships, deepen our work, and provide mutual support for our personal and professional growth.

On the final evening of each of our gatherings we come together for a special meal, followed by a time of sitting together in a circle, sharing stories from our work and our personal lives. Time dissolves during these circle gatherings, and we often continue into the early hours of the morning sharing our stories and funny anecdotes from past trainings, our poems and music, our triumphs and struggles with our careers, our hopes and visions, our joys and challenges with our own children and grandchildren, and our pleasures as well as painful losses with our families and relationships back home.

At one of our recent annual gatherings, a young Black teacher and doctoral student, who was a new member of our training team, shared the story of his mother's death a few months prior to our meeting. He told us that he had been the strong one in the family and had not yet been able to cry over the loss of his mother. As he spoke these words he broke into tears and cried deeply for several minutes, letting go of much pain held too long. As he cried, two other Black men held him and spoke quiet words of comfort. Those of us in the circle sat in silence, honoring this time, giving our support, and being thankful for the loving power of these two Black men engaged in healing their brother. When the young teacher regained his composure, he shared with the group that he had never before showed any deep personal emotions in the presence of White people. He was amazed that he had done so in this group and that he had felt supported in the process.

Our national trainer team is highly diverse. We are Black, White, Latino, Asian, American Indian, Aboriginal, Protestant, Catholic, Jewish, Buddhist,

Muslim, and Animist. We are older and younger, introverted and extro-
verted, male and female, straight and gay, variably stable and marginally
sane. We have many differences, yet we stand united in our common vision
and commitment to social transformation and healing. We work together
in highly stressful situations, and we relax and play together in the easy
way of lifelong friends. We have created a community of trust and mutual
respect wherein a young Black man (or any other member of our group)
can cry through his pain and find comfort and support in the privacy and
intimacy of his own racial group, as well as from a broader multicultural
family of colleagues. Our common commitment to education, equity, and
social justice is inspired and sustained by our immersion in this cauldron
of multicultural community.

After three decades in the embrace of this network, I know that this is
the kind of multicultural milieu from which our transformative vision and
healing work can and must emerge. I know we as educators and human
beings are able to create deep, productive, and committed connections
across our differences. And I know that the vision of a multicultural healing community is valid and attainable, because I and many others have
lived in such spaces for many years. None of us individually, and none of
our racial, ethnic, or cultural groups working in isolation, can accomplish
the enormous task of social healing that has been the focus of this book.
But by working together in committed communities of mutual respect and
support, there is no limit to our transformative possibilities.

BEYOND THE BORDERLANDS: *LA TIERRA TRANSFORMATIVA*

My colleagues in the REACH network are only a small part of a much
larger community of educators committed to the work of educational equity and social healing. There are many of us from all racial and cultural
groups throughout the world who have discovered both the dangers and
the delights on the river of diversity and who have learned to navigate its
often tumultuous waters. As a result of our commitment to personal and
social transformation, we have begun to populate a new land of multicultural consciousness, a place from which we nurture and sustain our vision
of educational and social change.

All of us who occupy this land of multicultural commitment have had
to cross the borders of our own particular identity groups to arrive in this
new mental, emotional, and political place. We have had to examine our
assumptions and challenge our fundamentalist and integrationist orientations. We have had to learn from each other, always open to unravel
ever-deeper layers of ignorance, narrowness, and defensiveness regard-

ing our limited perspectives and perceptions of truth. We have each had to broaden our doorways to truth, to allow more light into our personal and professional spaces, and to construct new homes along the river of diversity.

In the process of our work, we have discovered that this river eventually leads us to a new country, to a new place within our minds, hearts, and spirits, which I have chosen to call *La Tierra Transformativa,* the place of vision, healing, and positive change. Although I and many other writers (Anzaldua, 1987; Anzaldua & Keating, 2002; M. M. J. Fischer, 1986; Fregoso, 2003; Giroux, 1992; Griffin, 1995; hooks, 1990; Wellman, 1999) have used the language of the margins and the borderlands to describe our emergent transformational identity, it is perhaps time to acknowledge that we are no longer *merely* border dwellers. Perhaps we can now begin to move beyond this marginalized self-perception and claim the new land of multicultural vision, *La Tierra Transformativa,* as our legitimate home, as a new country we have already begun to create through our commitment to live in it. Through our common work and vision, educators representing all racial and cultural groups are beginning to inhabit this new multicultural space where the true spirit of equity reigns and where *E Pluribus Unum* is a lived reality.

We know that not everyone in our profession is willing or able at this time to join us in this new multicultural landscape. Many of our colleagues have other priorities and other commitments, and their imaginations will not necessarily be ignited by the fire of our vision for social justice. Not everyone is willing to suspend his or her culturally and politically prescribed certainties and embrace the credo of our new country, which is a credo of complexity and constant change and a commitment to keep our hearts and minds open to personal and social transformation.

We also know that significant social shifts are usually spearheaded by a relatively small number of visionary thinkers. In the struggle to heal the wounds of historical and contemporary dominance, racism, and oppression, only a few educators have chosen to carry the cause and hold the vision. These are the citizens of *La Tierra Transformativa,* who come from all racial and cultural groups and who have joined together in this new country of multicultural healing to carry out our work of social transformation. It is my hope that the population of this new country will continue to grow as we move through the first decades of the 21st century.

The work of transformationist educators is that of dismantling the dominance paradigm and healing the wounds of past and present racism. And beyond healing, our work is that of envisioning, creating, and modeling a better future, a new social paradigm that honors diversity and ensures greater equity for all of our people. Citizens of *La Tierra Transformativa* see "the choice to act as the real mission of living" (Derman-Sparks & Phillips, 1997, p. 158). We know that the true vision and action of multicultural education are identical to the vision of pluralistic democracy and the action of democratic citizenship (J. A. Banks, 2004; Giroux, 1997a; Nieto, 2005; Parker, 2003; Sleeter, 2001).

In the United States we have not yet achieved the full measure of equity, unity, justice, and opportunity that were envisioned by our Revolutionary thinkers and inscribed in our foundational principles. This is the "unfinished work" that inspired Lincoln's Second Inaugural Address. The unfinished work for transformationist educators is that of helping America *become* what America *says* it is. And beyond the United States, our responsibility is to join hands and share power with people everywhere who cry out for the ideals of pluralistic democracy, not as defined by us, but as envisioned by them.

I am particularly excited about the possibility of more White educators choosing to live and work in *La Tierra Transformativa*. As we learn to inhabit these multicultural spaces, we also come to know ourselves and our colleagues and students of color in new and deeper ways. From this richer foundation of knowing, it is then possible for us to grow toward greater authenticity and effectiveness in our teaching. This hope and this vision have inspired and sustained me in writing this book. As we have seen in the preceding chapters, there is much work that we as White educators must do to prepare ourselves for effective citizenship in this new land, but it is essential that we be represented there. Our responsibility as transformative teachers and citizens is to create for ourselves that social reality which we envision for others, to abandon the old landscapes of dominance, and to emigrate to those rich multicultural spaces where we can help change the world—one person, one school, one community, one nation at a time.

We know that the work of social transformation cannot be achieved by Whites alone, yet it cannot be achieved without us either. Both our percentage representation in the profession and our position in history require that a committed core of White educators become actively engaged in the creation of a new and healing multicultural reality, a new country of the heart, mind, and spirit where all people are welcomed with their differences intact. Together with our colleagues from other racial and cultural groups, we are now attempting to fashion a new and healthier way of being White. We are creating an activist and transformationist White identity both for ourselves and for a future generation of young students and teachers committed to social justice.

Guidelines for Discussion and Reflection

Introduction

1. "Why are they sending *these* kids to *our* school?" In what ways is this sentiment felt or expressed in your school district or institution? What groups of students are referred to in this way? How do you respond?
2. Do you think there is a causal relationship between the over-representation of White teachers in our nation's schools and the under-performance of students of color? Why or why not? What evidence supports your conclusion?
3. To what extent have you and your colleagues engaged in authentic and sustained conversation about issues of race and its influence in education? What would it take for you to talk together more openly and deeply about issues of race and other differences?
4. What are your concerns/hopes/expectations in reading this book? What questions to you have? Do you feel resistant or excited about continuing your reading? Share your thoughts and reactions with others in your discussion group.

Chapter 1: White Man Dancing

1. In what ways is the author's personal story similar to or different from the experiences of other White people you know?
2. What were the significant events/lessons/experiences that led Gary Howard to the work of multicultural education and social justice? How might other White people have responded differently to these same events or experiences?
3. What questions/challenges would you like to express to the author about his account of his personal journey?
4. What have been your own formative experiences related to race?

Chapter 2: White Dominance and the Weight of the West

1. What were your feelings/thoughts as you read the author's account of White social dominance as it affected Native Americans and Australian Aboriginals?
2. How is the experience of Indigenous peoples in relationship to social dominance similar to that of other racial/ethnic/cultural groups you are aware of? How is it unique?
3. What do you see as the relationship between social dominance and today's concerns about educational equity and closing the achievement gap?

Chapter 3: Decoding the Dominance Paradigm

1. Discuss and compare your understanding of the three dynamics of dominance: the Assumption of Rightness, the Luxury of Ignorance, and the Legacy of Privilege. What do these terms mean?
2. How do you see these three dynamics of dominance at play in classrooms, school systems, and the politics of education today?
3. What questions go unanswered and what issues go unresolved in the author's discussion of the dynamics of dominance in this chapter?
4. Where did you find yourself agreeing or disagreeing with Gary Howard's analysis of social dominance? Why?

Chapter 4: White Educators and the River of Change

1. In what ways does the metaphor of the river work or not work for you?
2. Compare and contrast your reactions to the author's four "healing responses": Honesty, Empathy, Advocacy, and Action. Are these the right responses for White educators and others to make in today's educational environment? Are they adequate? Are they what is needed in your school situation?
3. Discuss your different reactions to the author's statement on page 86: "I believe that systems of group-based inequality, which were originally established by choice and intent, can also be overcome through equally focused vision and will." What are the vision and the will needed to overcome inequities in public education? Is it possible?

4. Where do you see (or not see) evidence of this kind of vision at work in your own school and school district?

Chapter 5: Mapping the Journey of White Identity Development

1. In personal reflection, map the stages/steps in your own development related to the realities of race. How does the model presented by the author measure up to your own lived experience?
2. Together with colleagues, share stories about the significant experiences/stages in your racial identity development.
3. How do People of Color and White people experience racial identity development differently? What are the similarities?
4. How do you see issues of racial identity development impacting your students' lives?
5. What is the interplay between racial identity development and our work for educational equity? For us? For our students? For the larger community?

Chapter 6: Ways of Being White

1. How are tensions about race and "Whiteness" manifested in your schools? Among faculty? Administration? Parents? Students?
2. Discuss the different "ways of being White" described by the author in his White Identity Orientations model. Do you recognize people in these different stages? For White people, how do you see yourself reflected in these stages? For People of Color, how do you see these stages represented among your White colleagues?
3. What are the most important learnings/challenges/roadblocks/experiences for a White person in growing toward greater cultural competence and understanding of race?
4. How are these stages similar to or different from the experiences and challenges of People of Color in your growth toward racial authenticity?
5. What is the relationship between White Identity Orientations and student success? For your colleagues who are very effective at teaching across differences, how did they grow to that place of skill and competence?

Chapter 7: White Teachers and School Reform

1. Do you agree with Gary Howard's assertion that the achievement gap in education today is, in many ways, the result of our history of White social dominance? What evidence to you see that either supports or counters his argument?
2. Discuss the elements of *knowing* and *doing* that Gary Howard incorporates into his description of transformationist teaching. Select one of the elements that particularly speaks to you—and share your thoughts/reflections about this element with others in your discussion group.
3. Reflect on Figures 7.1, 7.2, and 7.3. How do these models relate to your own teaching/leadership? What is helpful about these designs? What is missing?

Chapter 8: Our Unfinished Work

1. What was your reaction to the Gary Howard's description of "the place of vision, healing, and positive change"?
2. For People of Color and White people, what do we need from each other if we are to create spaces of trust and effective collaboration in the service of our students?
3. What are the barriers to the creation of this place the author calls *La Tierra Transformativa*? What dues must we each pay to enter this space?
4. How do we (can we) move beyond shame and blame and actually create schools as places of hope and healing?
5. Together with your colleagues, map the contours of your own vision of *La Tierra Transformativa*. What does that place look like where we and our schools are transformed in such a way that we successfully serve all of our students well? How will we know it when we see it?

References

Alba, R. D. (1990). *Ethnic identity: The transformation of White America.* New Haven, CT: Yale University Press.

Allen, P. G. (1992). *The sacred hoop: Recovering the feminine in American Indian traditions.* Boston: Beacon.

Allen, R. L. (1999). *The hidden curriculum of Whiteness: White teachers, White territory, and White community.* Los Angeles: UCLA Graduate School of Education.

Anyon, J. (1997). *Ghetto schooling: A political economy of urban educational reform.* New York: Teachers College Press.

Anzaldua, G. (1987). *Borderlands/LaFrontera: The New Mestiza.* San Francisco: Spinsters/Aunt Lute.

Anzaldua, G., & Keating, A. (2002). *This bridge we call home: Radical visions for transformation.* New York: Routledge.

Apple, M. W. (1997). Consuming the other: Whiteness, education, and cheap french fries. In M. Fine, L. Weis, L. Powell, & L. Wang (Eds.), *Off white: Readings on race, power, and society* (pp. 121–128). New York: Routledge.

Apple, M. W. (2000). *Official knowledge* (2nd ed.). New York: Routledge.

Apple, M. W., Aasen, P., Cho, M. K., Gandin, L. A., Oliver, A., & Sung, Y. K. (2003). *The state and the politics of knowledge.* New York: Routledge Falmer.

Applebaum, B. (2000). "On good authority or is feminist authority an oxymoron?" In R. Curren, *Philosophy of education* (pp. 307–317). Urbana-Champaign, IL: Philosophy of Education Society.

Appleby, J. (1992). Recovering America's historic diversity: Beyond exceptionalism. *The Journal of American History, 79*(2), 419–431.

Aronson, J. (2004, November). The threat of stereotype. *Educational Leadership, 62*(3), 14–19.

Aronson, J., & Steele, C. M. (2005). Stereotypes and the fragility of human competence, motivation, and self-concept. In C. Dweck & E. Elliot (Eds.), *Handbook of competence and motivation.* New York: Guilford.

Banks, C. A. M. (2005). *Improving multicultural education: Lessons from the intergroup education movement.* New York: Teachers College Press.

Banks, C. A. M., & Banks, J. A. (1995, Summer). Equity pedagogy: An essential component of multicultural education. *Theory Into Practice, 34*(3), 152–158.

Banks, J. A. (1994). *Multiethnic education: Theory and practice* (3rd ed.). Needham Heights, MA: Allyn & Bacon.

Banks, J. A. (1996). The historical reconstruction of knowledge about race: Implications for transformative teaching. In J. A. Banks (Ed.), *Multicultural education, transformative knowledge, and action* (pp. 64–87). New York: Teachers College Press.

Banks, J. A. (1997). *Educating citizens in a multicultural society.* New York: Teachers College Press.

Banks, J. A. (2004). Multicultural education: Historical development, dimensions, and practice. In J. A. Banks & C. A. M. Banks, *Handbook of research on multicultural education* (2nd Ed., pp. 3–29). San Francisco: Jossey-Bass.

Banks, J. A. (2006). Series foreword. In E. Garcia, *Teaching and learning in two languages: Bilingualism and schooling in the United States* (pp. vii–xi). New York: Teachers College Press.

Banks, J. A., & Banks, C. A. M. (2005). *Handbook of research on multicultural education* (2nd Ed.). San Francisco: Jossey-Bass.

Barton, P. E. (2004, November). Why does the gap persist? *Educational Leadership, 62*(3). 9–13.

Bishop, A. (1994). *Becoming an ally: Breaking the cycle of oppression.* Halifax, Nova Scotia: Fernwood.

Bishops' apology. (1987). Seattle: Washington Association of Churches.

Bourne, R. S. (1916, July). Trans-national America. *The Atlantic Monthly, 11,* 86–97.

Boyd, B. A., & Correa, V. I. (2005). Developing a framework for reducing cultural clash between African American parents and the special education system. *Multicultural Perspectives, 7*(2), 3–11.

Broome, R. (1982). *Aboriginal Australians: Black response to white dominance 1788–1980.* Sydney: Allen & Unwin.

Butler, J. (1990). *Awash in a sea of faith: Christianizing the American people.* Cambridge, MA: Harvard University Press.

Cajete, G. (1993). *Look to the mountain: An ecology of indigenous education.* Norwood, CO: Kivaki Press.

Campbell, D. T. (1967). Stereotypes and the perception of group differences. *American Psychologist, 22,* 817–829.

Carlson, D. (1997). Stories of colonial and postcolonial education. In M. Fine, L. Weis, L. Powell, & L. Wang (Eds.), *Off White: Readings on race, power, and society* (pp. 137–148). New York: Routledge.

Carter, R. T. (1995). *The influence of race and racial identity in psychotherapy: Toward a racially inclusive model.* New York: Wiley.

Chase A. (1977). *The legacy of Malthus: The social costs of the new scientific racism.* New York: Knopf.

Chavez-Chavez, C. R., & O'Donnell, J. (Eds.). (1998). *Speaking the unpleasant: The politics of (non)engagement in the multicultural education terrain.* Albany: State University of New York Press.

Clark, C. R., & O'Donnell, J. (Eds.). (1999). *Becoming and unbecoming White: Owning and disowning a racial identity.* Westport, CT: Greenwood Press.

Clark, K. B., & Clark, M. P. (1947). Racial identification and preferences in Negro children. In T. Newcomb & E. L. Hartley (Eds.), *Readings in social psychology* (pp. 551–560). New York: Holt.

Cochran-Smith, M., Davis, D., & Fries, K. (2004). Multicultural teacher education: Research, practice, and policy. In J. A. Banks & C. A. M. Banks, *Handbook of research on multicultural education* (2nd Ed.; pp. 939–978). San Francisco: Jossey-Bass.

Code, L. (1991). *What can she know? Feminist theory and the construction of knowledge.* Ithaca, NY: Cornell University Press.

Cole, S. G., & Cole, M. W. (1954). *Minorities and the American promise.* New York: Harper.

Comer, J. P. (1988, November). Educating poor minority children. *Scientific American, 259*(5), 42–48.

Comer, J. P. (2004). *Leave no child behind: Preparing today's youth for tomorrow's world.* New Haven, CT: Yale University Press.

Congressional Globe. (1846). Washington, DC.

Cookson, P. W., Jr. (1991, February). Private schooling and equity: Dilemmas of choice. *Education and Urban Society, 23*(2), 185–199.

Cross, W. E., Jr. (1971). The Negro to Black conversion experience: Toward a psychology of Black liberation. *Black World, 20*(9), 13–27.

Cross, W. E., Jr. (1978). Models of psychological nigresence. *Journal of Black Psychology, 5*(1), 13–31.

Cross, W. E., Jr. (1991). *Shades of black: Diversity in African-American identity.* Philadelphia: Temple University Press.

Darder, A. (1991). *Culture and power in the classroom: A critical foundation for bicultural education.* Westport, CT: Bergin & Garvey.

Darder, A. (2002). *Reinventing Paulo Freire: A pedagogy of love.* Boulder, CO: Westview Press.

Darling-Hammond, L. (2004). What happens to a dream deferred? The continuing question for equal educational opportunity. In J. A. Banks & C. A. M. Banks, *Handbook of research on multicultural education* (2nd Ed.; pp. 607–630). San Francisco: Jossey-Bass.

Deloria, V., Jr. (1974). *Behind the trail of broken treaties: An Indian declaration of independence.* New York: Delacorte.

Deloria, V., Jr. (1991). *Indian education in America.* Boulder, CO: American Indian Science and Engineering Society.

Delpit, L. (1996). *Other people's children: Cultural conflict in the classroom.* New York: The New Press.

Delpit, L. (2002). *The skin we speak.* New York: The New Press.

Dennis, R. M. (1981). Socialization and racism: The White experience. In B. P. Bowser & R. G. Hunt (Eds.), *Impacts of racism on White Americans* (pp. 71–85). Beverly Hills, CA: Sage.

Derman-Sparks, L., & Phillips, C. B. (1997). *Teaching/learning anti-racism: A developmental approach.* New York: Teachers College Press.

Dupris, J. C. (1979). The national impact of multicultural education: A renaissance of Native American culture through tribal self-determination and Indian control of education. In *Multicultural education and the American Indian* (pp. 43–54). Los Angeles: University of California, American Indian Studies Center.

Eck, D. L. (2001). *A new religious America: How a "Christian country" has become the world's most religiously diverse nation.* New York: Harper.

Education Trust. (2002). *Dispelling the myth revisited: Preliminary findings from a nationwide analysis of high-flying schools* (P. Noguera, Ed.). Washington, DC: Author.

Elmore, R. (2002). *Bridging the gap between standards and achievement.* Washington, DC: Albert Shanker Institute.

Emerson, L. (1997, March 7). *Traditional views on Native American retention in schools.* Paper presented to the Cultural Advocates for Nations at Risk Project, San Diego State University.

Erikson, E. H. (1963). *Childhood and society.* New York: Norton. (Original work published 1950)

Ferguson, A. A. (2000). *Bad boys: Public schools in the making of Black masculinity.* Ann Arbor: University of Michigan Press.

Ferguson, R. (2000). *A diagnostic analysis of black-white GPA disparities in Shaker Heights, Ohio.* Washington, DC: Brookings Institute.

Fields, B. (1990). Slavery, race, and ideology in the United States of America. *New Left Review, 181,* 95–118.

Fierros, E., & Conroy, J. (2001). Double jeopardy: An exploration of restrictiveness and race in special education. In. D. Olsen & G. Orfield (Eds.), *Racial inequity in special education* (pp. 39–70). Boston: Harvard Education Press.

Fine, M., Weiss, L., Powell, L., & Wong, L. (Eds.). (1997). *Off white: Readings on race, power, and society.* New York: Routledge.

Fischer, C. S., Hout, M., Jankowski, M. S., Lucas, S. R., Swidler, A., & Voss, K. (1996). *Inequality by design: Cracking the bell curve myth.* Princeton, NJ: Princeton University Press.

Fischer, M. M. J. (1986). Ethnicity and the post-modern arts of memory. In J. Clifford & G. E. Marcus (Eds.), *Writing culture: The poetics and politics of ethnography* (pp. 194–233). Berkeley: University of California Press.

Fiske, J. (1989). *Reading the popular.* Boston: Unwin & Hyman.

Franklin, J. H. (1976). *Racial equality in America.* Columbia: University of Missouri Press.

Fregoso, R. L. (2003). *MeXicana encounters: The making of social identities on the borderlands.* Berkeley: University of California Press.

Freire, P. (1970). *Pedagogy of the oppressed.* New York: Herder & Herder.

Freire, P. (2004). *Pedagogy of hope: Reliving pedagogy of the oppressed.* New York: Continuum International Publishing Group.

Fuchs, E., & Havinghurst, R. J. (1973). *To live on this earth: American Indian education.* New York: Doubleday.

Gaertner, S. L. (1976). Nonreactive measures in racial attitude research: A focus on "liberals." In P. A. Katz (Ed.), *Towards the elimination of racism* (pp.

183–211). New York: Pergamon.

Ganter, G. (1977). The socio-conditions of the white practitioner: New perspectives. *Journal of Contemporary Psychotherapy, 9*(1), 26–32.

Garcia, E. (2005, March). *Teaching and learning in two languages: Bilingualism and schooling in the United States.* New York: Teachers College Press.

Gates, H. L., Jr. (1997, April 11). *Race and class in America.* Speech delivered at the University of Washington, Seattle.

Gay, G. (2000). *Culturally responsive teaching: Theory, research, and practice.* New York: Teachers College Press.

Gay, G., Dingus, J. E., & Jackson, C. W. (2003, July). The presence and performance of teachers of color in the profession. Unpublished report prepared for the National Collaborative on Diversity in the Teaching Force. Washington, DC.

Giroux, H. A. (1992). *Border crossings: Cultural workers and the politics of education.* New York: Routledge.

Giroux, H. A. (1997a). Pedagogy and the politics of hope: Theory, culture, and schooling. Boulder, CO: Westview.

Giroux, H. A. (1997b, Summer). Rewriting the discourse of racial identity: Towards a pedagogy and politics of Whiteness. *Harvard Educational Review, 67*(2), 285–320.

Gomez, M. L. (1996). Prospective teachers' perspectives on teaching "Other people's children." In K. Zeichner, S. Melnick, & M. L. Gomez (Eds.), *Currents of reform in preservice teacher education* (pp. 109–132). New York: Teachers College Press.

Gould, S. J. (1981). *The mismeasure of man.* New York: Norton.

Gramsci, A. (1972). *Selections from the prison notebooks* (Q. Hoare & G. Smith, Eds.). New York: Irvington.

Green, T., McIntosh, A., Cook-Morales, V. J., & Robinson-Zañarta, C. (2005). From old schools to tomorrow's schools: Psychoeducational assessment of African American students. *Remedial and Special Education, 26*(2), 82–92.

Griffin, G. B. (1995). *Season of the witch.* Pasadena: Triology Books.

Grossman, K. N., Beaupre, B., & Rossi, R. (2001, Sept. 7). Poorest kids often wind up with the weakest teachers. *Chicago Sun Times.*

Hale, J E. (2004, November). How schools shortchange African American children. *Educational Leadership, 62*(3), 34–39.

Hall, S. (1996). New ethnicities. In D. Morley & K-H. Chen (Eds.), *Stuart Hall: Critical dialogues in cultural studies.* New York: Routledge.

Hardiman, R. (1979). *White identity development theory.* Unpublished manuscript.

Hardy, R. D. (2004, April). The new diversity: Demographic shifts since *Brown* are changing the face of America's racial and ethnic landscape. *American School Board Journal, 191*(4), 40–44.

Harvey, K. D., & Harjo, L. D. (1994). *Indian country: A history of native people in America.* Golden, CO: North American Press.

Havinghurst, R. J. (1978). The education of American Indian children and youth (Summary report and recommendations: *National Study of American Indian*

Education, Series No. 4, No. 6). Minneapolis: University of Minnesota.

Haycock, K. (2004, Winter). The real value of teachers: If good teachers matter, why don't we act like it? *Thinking K-16* [A publication of the Education Trust], *8*(1), 1–2.

Hebbeler, K., Wagner, M., Spiker, D., Scarborough, A., Simeonsson, R., & Collier, M. (2001). *A first look at the characteristics of children and families entering early intervention services.* Menlo Park, CA: SRI International.

Helms, J. E. (1984). Toward an explanation of the influence of race in the counseling process: A black-white model. *The Counseling Psychologist, 12,* 153–165.

Helms, J. E. (Ed.). (1990). *Black and White racial identity: Theory, research, and practice.* Westport, CT: Greenwood Press.

Helms, J. E. (1992). *Race is a nice thing to have.* Topeka, KS: Content Communications.

Helms, J. E. (1994). Racial identity and "racial" constructs. In E. J. Trickett, R. Watts, & D. Birman (Eds.), *Human diversity* (pp. 285–311). San Francisco: Jossey-Bass.

Helms, J. E. (1996). Toward a methodology for measuring and assessing racial as distinguished from ethnic identity. In G. R. Sodowsky & J. C. Impara (Eds.), *Multicultural assessment in counseling and clinical psychology* (pp. 143–192). Lincoln, NE: Buros Institute of Mental Measurements.

Helms, J. E., & Piper, R. E. (1994). Implications of racial identity theory for vocational psychology. *Journal of Vocational Behavior, 44,* 124–138.

Herrnstein, R. J., & Murray, C. (1994). *The bell curve: Intelligence and class structure in the American life.* New York: Free Press.

Hinkle, S., & Brown, R. (1990). Intergroup comparisons and social identity: Some links and lacunae. In D. Abrams & M. Hogg (Eds.), *Advances in social identity theory* (pp. 48–70). New York: Springer Verlag.

Hodgkinson, H. (1991). Reform versus reality. *Phi Delta Kappan, 73*(1), 9–16.

Hodgkinson, H. (2001). Educational demographics: What teachers should know. *Educational Leadership, 58*(4), 6–11.

Hodgkinson, H. (2002). Demographics and teacher education. *Journal of Teacher Education, 53*(2), 102–105.

Holmstrom, D. (1997, January 30). Two of drama's great feuds over Black theater in America. *Christian Science Monitor,* p. 15.

hooks, b. (1990). *Yearning: Race, gender, and cultural politics.* Boston: South End Press.

Horsman, R. (1981). *Race and manifest destiny.* Cambridge, MA: Harvard University Press.

Howard, G. R. (1993). Whites in multicultural education: Rethinking our role. *Phi Delta Kappan, 75*(1), 36–41.

Howard, G. R. (2002, Spring). School improvement for all: Reflections on the achievement gap. *Journal for School Improvement, 3*(1), 11–17.

Howard, G. R. (2004, Fall). How we are white. *Teaching Tolerance, 26,* 50–52.

Howard, L., & Rothbart, M. (1980). Social categorization and memory for ingroup and out-group behavior. *Journal of Personality and Social Psychology, 38,* 301–310.

Hughes, L. (1994). The Negro speaks of rivers. In *The collected poems of Langston*

Hughes. New York: Alfred A. Knopf. (Original work published in 1921)

Ignatiev, N. (1996). Editorial. In N. Ignatiev & J. Garvey (Eds.), *Race traitor* (pp. 9–14). New York: Routledge.

Jackman, M. R. (1981). Education and policy commitment to racial integration. *American Journal of Political Science, 25*(2), 256–269.

Jencks, C., & Phillips, M. (1998). *The black-white test scores gap*. Washington, DC: Brookings Institute.

Joe, J. R. (1994). Revaluing Native American concepts of development and education. In P. M. Greenfield & R. R. Cocking (Eds.), *Cross-cultural roots of minority child development* (pp. 107–113). Hillsdale, NJ: Erlbaum.

Johnson, A. G. (2001). *Privilege, power and difference*. New York: McGraw-Hill.

Johnston, B. (1995). *The Manitous: The supernatural world of the Ojibway*. New York: HarperCollins.

Jonas, S. (1991). *The battle for Guatemala: Rebels, death squads and U.S. power*. Boulder, CO: Westview.

Jones, J. M. (1972). *Prejudice and racism*. New York: Random House.

Katz, D. (1960). The functional approach to the study of attitudes. *Public Opinion Quarterly, 24*, 163–204.

Katz, J. H., & Ivey, A. E. (1977). White awareness: The frontier of racism awareness training. *Personnel and Guidance Journal, 55*(18), 485–488.

Keeley, E. F. (1996). *Racism undercover in the suburbs*. Souderton, PA: Diversity Dialogue Press.

Kelves, D. J. (1985). *In the name of eugenics: Genetics and the use of human heredity*. New York: Knopf.

Kidder, L. H. (1997). Colonial remnants: Assumptions of privilege. In M. Fine, L. Weis, L. Powell, & L. Wang (Eds.), *Off White: Readings on race, power, and society* (pp. 158–166). New York: Routledge.

King, J. E. (1991). Dysconscious racism: Ideology, identity, and the mis-education of teachers. *Journal of Negro Education, 60*(2), 133–146.

Kingsolver, B. (1995). *High tide in Tucson*. New York: HarperCollins.

Kivel, P. (2002). *Uprooting racism: How White people can work for racial justice* (Rev. Ed.). Philadelphia: New Society Publishers.

Klein, N. (2005, May 2). The rise of disaster capitalism. *The Nation*, 9–11.

Kleinfeld, J. (1975, February). Effective teachers of Eskimo and Indian students. *School Review, 83*(2), 301–344.

Kovel, J. S. (1970). *White racism: A psychohistory*. New York: Pantheon.

Kozol, J. (1991). *Savage inequalities*. New York: Crown.

Kozol, J. (2005). *The shame of the nation: The restoration of Apartheid schooling in America*. New York: Crown.

Kriesberg, S. (1992). *Transforming power: Domination, empowerment, and education*. Albany: State University of New York Press.

Ladson-Billings, G. (1994). *The dreamkeepers. Successful teachers of African American students*. San Francisco: Jossey-Bass.

Ladson-Billings, G. (2001, Summer). Teaching and cultural competence: What does it take to be a successful teacher in a diverse classroom? *Rethinking Schools, 15*(4), 16–18.

Ladson-Billings, G. (2002). *Crossing over to Canaan: The journey of new teachers in diverse classrooms.* San Francisco: Jossey-Bass.

Lawrence-Lightfoot, S. (2003). *The essential conversation: What parents and teachers can learn from each other.* Random House: New York.

Leach, M. M., Behrens, J. T., & LaFleur, N. K. (2002, April). White racial identity and White racial consciousness: Similarities, differences, and recommendations. *Journal of Multicultural Counseling and Development, 30*(2), 66–80.

Levine, L. (1996). *The opening of the American mind.* Boston: Beacon.

Lewis, A. (2003). *Race in the school yard: Negotiating the color-line in classrooms and communities.* New York: Rutgers University Press.

Lewis, J. E. (1996). *The West: The making of the American West.* New York: Carroll & Graf.

Locust, C. (1988). Wounding the spirit: Discrimination and traditional American Indian belief systems. *Harvard Educational Review, 58*(3), 315–330.

Mabo v. Queensland (No. 2). (1992). *Australian Commonwealth Law Report No. 1.* Canberra: Australia Government Publishers.

MacLeod, A. (1997, April 28). Last shards of its empire: Jab at modern, downsized Britain. *Christian Science Monitor,* pp. 1, 8.

Males, M. (1996). *The scapegoat generation.* Monroe, ME: Common Courage Press.

Maslow, A. H. (1962). *Toward a psychology of being.* Princeton, NJ: Van Nostrand.

Mathis, W. J. (2003, May). No Child Left Behind: Cost and benefits. *Phi Delta Kappan, 84*(9), 679–685.

McIntosh, P. (1988). White privilege and male privilege: A personal account of coming to see correspondences through work in women's studies. In M. L. Andersen & P. Hill-Collins (Eds.), *Race, class, and gender: An anthology* (pp. 70–81). Wellesley, MA: Wellesley College Center for Research on Women.

McIntosh, P. (1989, July/August). White privilege: Unpacking the invisible knapsack. *Peace and Freedom,* pp. 10–12.

McKinley, J. H. (2005, March). *Culturally responsive teaching and learning.* Paper presented at the 13th annual state conference of the Washington Alliance of Black School Educators, Bellevue, WA.

McLaren, P. (1988, Fall). On ideology and education: Critical pedagogy and the politics of education. *Social Text, 19–20,* pp. 153–185.

McLuhan, T. C. (1971). *Touch the earth: A self-portrait of Indian existence.* New York: Promontory Press.

McNeil, L. (2000). *Contradictions of school reform: Educational cost of standardized testing.* New York: Routledge.

McShane, D. (1983). Explaining achievement patterns of American Indian children: A transcultural and developmental model. *Peabody Journal of Education, 61,* 34–48.

Meier, D., & Wood, G. H. (Eds.). (2005). *Many children left behind: How the No Child Left Behind Act is damaging our children and our schools.* Boston: Beacon.

Mitchell, T. L. (1839). *Three expeditions into the interior of eastern Australia, Vol II.* London: T. W. Boone

Moll, L. C. (1991). Social and instructional issues in literacy instruction for "disadvantaged" students. In M. S. Knapp & P. M. Shields (Eds.), *Better schooling for children of poverty: Alternatives to conventional wisdom* (pp. 61–84). Berkeley, CA: McCutchan.

Moll, L. C., & Gonzaléz, N. (2004). Engaging life: A funds-of-knowledge approach to multicultural education. In J. A. Banks & C. A. M. Banks, *Handbook of research on multicultural education* (2nd Ed.; pp. 699–715). San Francisco: Jossey-Bass.

Montagu, A. (1997). *Race, man's most dangerous myth: The fallacy of race.* Walnut Creek, CA: Altamira Press. (Original work published 1942)

Morefield, J. (1996). *Recreating schools for all children.* Retrieved June 10, 2005 from http://newhorizons.org/article_morefield.html

Mukhopadhyay, C., & Henze, R. C. (2003, May). How real is race? Using anthropology to make sense of human diversity. *Phi Delta Kappan, 84*(9), 669–678.

National Center for Educational Statistics, U.S. Department of Health, Education, and Welfare. (1996). *Digest of educational statistics.* Washington, DC: GPO.

National Center for Educational Statistics, U.S. Department of Health, Education, and Welfare. (2003). *The nation's report card.* Washington, DC: GPO.

National Center for Educational Statistics. (2003). *National assessment of educational progress. The nation's report card: 2003 mathematics and reading results.* Available online at: http://nces.ed.gov/nationsreportcard/reading/results 2003/raceethnicity.asp

National Collaborative on Diversity in the Teaching Force, U.S. (2004). *Assessment of diversity in the America's teaching force: A call to action.* Washington, DC: National Collaborative.

National Education Association. (2003, August). *Status of the American public school teacher 2000–2001.* Washington, DC: NEA Research.

Neville, H. A., Lilly, R. L., Duran, G., Lee, R. M., & Growne, L. (2000). Construction and initial validation of the color-blind racial attitudes scale (CoBRAS). *Journal of Counseling Psychology, 47,* 59–70.

Nickerson, C. (1996, November 22). Independence for Canadian Indians urged. *Seattle Times,* p. 1.

Nieto, S. (1996). *Affirming diversity: The socio-political content of multicultural education* (2nd ed.). White Plains, NY: Longman.

Nieto, S. (1998). From claiming hegemony to sharing space: Creating community in multicultural courses. In R. Chavez & J. O'Donnell (Eds.), *Speaking the unpleasant: The politics of (non)engagement in the multicultural education terrain* (pp. 16–31). Albany: State University of New York Press.

Nieto, S. (1999). *The light in their eyes: Creating multicultural learning communities.* New York: Teachers College Press.

Nieto, S. (2003). *What keeps teachers going?* New York: Teachers College Press.

Nieto. S. (2004). Black, White, and us: The meaning of *Brown v. Board of Education* for Latinos. *Multicultural Perspectives, 6*(4), 3–5.

Nieto, S. (2005a). Social justice in hard times: Celebrating the vision of Dr. Martin Luther King, Jr. *Multicultural Perspectives, 7*(1), 3–7.

Nieto, S. (2005b). *Why we teach.* New York: Teachers College Press.

Noguera, P. (2003). *City schools and the American dream: Reclaiming the promise of public education.* New York: Teachers College Press.

Novick, M. (1995). *White lies, White power: The fight against White supremacy and reactionary violence.* Monroe, ME: Common Courage Press.

O'Brien, S. (1889). *American Indian tribal governments.* Norman: University of Oklahoma Press.

O'Donohue, J. (2004). *Beauty: The invisible embrace.* New York: HarperCollins.

Omi, M., & Winant, H. (1986). *Racial formation in the United States.* New York: Routledge.

Omi, M., & Winant, H. (1993). On the theoretical status of the concept of race. In C. McCarthy & W. Crichlow (Eds.), *Race, identity, and representation in education* (pp. 3–10). New York: Routledge.

Orfield, G., & Eaton, S. (1996). *Dismantling desegregation: The quiet reversal of Brown v. Board of Education.* New York: The New Press.

Orfield, G., & Lee, C. (2004, January). *Brown* at 50: King's dream or *Plessy's* nightmare? Report of the Civil Rights Project at Harvard University.

Paley, V. G. (1979). *White teacher.* Cambridge, MA: Harvard University Press.

Paley, V. G. (2000, March). *White teacher (New Preface).* Cambridge, MA: Harvard University Press.

Palmer, P. (1998). *Courage to teach.* San Francisco: Jossey-Bass.

Palmer, P. (2000). *Let your life speak: Listening for the voice of vocation.* San Francisco: Jossey-Bass.

Parham, T. A. (1989). Cycles of psychological nigresence. *The Counseling Psychologist, 17,* 187–226.

Parker, W. (2003). *Teaching democracy: Unity and diversity in the public life.* New York: Teachers College Press.

Peach, B. (Producer). (1984). *The explorers.* New York: ABC.

Pence, D. J., & Fields, J. A. (1999, April). Teaching about race and ethnicity: Trying to uncover White privilege for a White audience. *Teaching Sociology, 27*(2), 150–158.

Prucha, F. P. (1975). *Documents of United States Indian policy.* Lincoln: University of Nebraska Press.

Reed, P. (1982). *The stolen generations: The removal of Aboriginal children in N.S.W. 1883–1969.* Sydney: New South Wales Ministry of Aboriginal Affairs.

Reif-Hulser, M. (1999). *Borderlands: Negotiating boundaries in post-colonial writing.* Amsterdam: Rodopi.

Resnick, L. B., & Harwell, M. (1998, March). *High performance learning communities: District #2 achievement* [A report to the Office of Educational Research and Improvement]. Pittsburgh, PA: University of Pittsburgh, Learning Research and Development Center.

Resnick, L. B., & Johnson, A. (1988). Intelligent machines for intelligent people: Cognitive theory and the future of the computer-assisted learning. In R. S. Nickerson & P. P. Zodhiates (Eds.), *Technology in education: Looking toward*

2020 (pp. 139–168). Hillsdale, NJ: Erlbaum.

Reyhner, J., & Eder, J. (1989). *A history of Indian education.* Billings, MT: Native American Studies, Eastern Montana College.

Reynolds, R. J. (2005). The education of indigenous Australian students: Same story, different hemisphere. *Multicultural Perspectives, 7*(2), 48–55.

Rist, R. C. (1974). Race, policy and schooling. *Society, 12*(1), 59–63.

Robinson, M., Robinson-Zañartu, C., Honanie, E., Hunt, T., & Zamora, E. (2004, June). *Decolonizing issues in the education of Native American Students.* Invited presentation to the 9th annual Conference on Gifted/Talented and Exceptional Education for Native People, San Diego.

Robinson-Zañartu, C. (1996, October). Serving Native American children and families: Considering cultural variables. *Language, Speech, and Hearing Services in Schools, 27*(4), 373–384.

Robinson-Zañartu, C. (2003). *Native American scholars and collaborators.* Washington, DC: U.S. Department of Education, Office of Special Education.

Rodriquez, N. M., & Villaverde, L. (2000). *Dismantling White privilege: Pedagogy, politics and Whiteness* (Counterpoints: Studies in the Postmodern Theory of Education, Vol. 73.). New York: Peter Lang Publishing.

Roediger, D. (1994). *Towards the abolition of Whiteness.* London: Verso.

Rosaldo, R. (1989). *Culture and truth: The remaking of social analysis.* Boston: Beacon.

Rosenthal, R. (2002). The Pygmalion effect and its mediating mechanisms. In J. Aronson (Ed.), *Improving academic achievement: Impact of psychological factors on education.* San Diego, CA: Academic Press.

Rothbart, M., & John, O. P. (1993). Intergroup relations and stereotype change: A social-cognitive analysis of some longitudinal findings. In P. M. Sniderman, P. E. Tetlock, & E. G. Carmines (Eds.), *Prejudice, politics and the American dilemma* (pp. 32–59). Stanford, CA: Stanford University Press.

Rowley, C. D. (1970). *The destruction of Aboriginal society.* Ringwood, Australia: Penguin.

Rushdie, S. (1997, August 11). India at five-O. *Time,* pp. 40–42.

Schlafly, P. (1984). *Child abuse in the classroom.* Alton, IL: Pere Marquette Press.

Schofield, J. W. (1997). Causes and consequences of the colorblind perspective. In J. A. Banks & C. A. M. Banks (Eds.), *Multicultural education: Issues and perspectives* (3rd ed.; pp. 251–271). Boston: Allyn & Bacon.

Schofield, J. W. (2000). The colorblind perspective's impact on intergroup relations. In J. A. Banks & C. A. M. Banks (Eds.), *Multicultural education: Issues and perspectives* (4th ed.; pp. 247–267). New York: John Wiley & Sons.

Secada, W. G. (1991). Selected conceptual and methodological issues for studying the mathematics education of the disadvantaged. In M. S. Knapp & P. M. Shields (Eds.), *Better schooling for children of poverty: Alternatives to conventional wisdom* (pp. 61–84). Berkeley, CA: McCutchan.

Shade, B. J., Kelly, C., & Oberg, M. (1997). *Creating culturally responsive classrooms.* Washington, DC.: American Psychological Association.

Sheets, R. H. (2000, December). Advancing the field or taking the center stage: The white movement in multicultural education. *Educational Researcher, 29*(9), 15–21.

Sidanius, J., & Pratto, F. (1993). The inevitability of oppression and the dynamics of social dominance. In P. M. Sniderman, P. E. Tetlock, & E. G. Carmines (Eds.), *Prejudice, politics and the American dilemma* (pp. 173–211). Stanford, CA: Stanford University Press.

Sleeter, C. E. (1994). White racism. *Multicultural Education, 1*(4), 5–8, 39.

Sleeter, C. E. (1996). *Multicultural education as social activism.* Albany: State University of New York Press.

Sleeter, C. (1999[1996]) Teaching whites about racism. In E. Lee, D. Menkart & M. Okazawa-Rey (Eds.), *Beyond heroes and holidays: A practical guide to K–12 anti-racist, multicultural education and staff development* (pp. 36–44). Washington DC: Network of Educators on the Americas.

Sleeter, C. E. (2001). *Culture, difference, and power.* New York: Teachers College Press.

Sleeter, C. E. (2006). *Un-standardizing curriculum: Multicultural teaching in standards-based curriculum.* New York: Teachers College Press.

Sniderman, P. M., Tetlock, P., & Carmines, E. G. (Eds.). (1993). *Prejudice, politics, and the American dilemma.* Stanford, CA: Stanford University Press.

Solidarity Foundation. (1996, Spring). Pulling the land out from under Brazil's Indigenous peoples. *Native Americans, 13*(1), 12–13.

Steele, C. M. (2004). A threat in the air: How stereotypes shape intellectual identity and performance. In J. A. Banks & C. A. M. Banks (Eds.), *Handbook of research on multicultural education* (pp. 682–698). San Francisco: Jossey-Bass.

Tajfel, H. (1970). Experiments in intergroup discrimination. *Scientific American, 233*(5), 96–102.

Tatum, B. C. (1992, Spring). Talking about race, learning about racism: The application of racial identity theory in the classroom. *Harvard Educational Review, 62*(1), 321–348.

Tatum, B. C. (2003). *Why are all the black kids sitting together in the cafeteria? And other conversations about race* (5th ed.). New York: Basic Books.

Tillich, P. (1966). *On the boundary: An autobiographical sketch.* New York: Scribners.

Thernstrom, A., & Thernstrom, S. (2003). *No excuses: Closing the racial gap in learning.* New York: Simon and Schuster.

Todorov, T. (1982). *The conquest of America: The question of the other.* New York: HarperCollins.

Vasquez, J. A. (1988). Contexts of learning for minority students. *Educational Forum, 52*(3), 243–253.

Vavrus, M. (2002). *Transforming the multicultural education of teachers: Theory, research and practice.* New York: Teachers College Press.

Vogel, V. J. (1972). *This country was ours: A documentary history of the American Indian.* New York: Harper & Row.

Wall, C. A. (1989). Taking positions and changing words. In C. A. Wall (Ed.), *Changing our own words: Essays on criticism, theory, and writing by Black women* (pp. 1–15). New Brunswick, NJ: Rutgers University Press.

Ward, G. C. (1996). *The West: An illustrated history.* Boston: Little, Brown.

Weinberg, M. (1991). *Racism in the United States: A comprehensive classified bibliography.* Westport, CT: Greenwood.

Weinberg, B. (1996, Summer). Land and sovereignty in Hawai'i: A native nation re-emerges. *Native Americans, 13*(2), 30–41.

Weinstein, R. S. (2002). *Reaching higher: The power of expectations in schooling.* Cambridge, MA: Harvard University Press.

Weiss, L., & Fine, M. (2003). *Excavating race, class, and gender among urban youth.* New York: Teachers College Press.

Weiss, L., Proweller, A., & Centrie, C. (1997). Re-examining "A moment in history": Loss of privilege inside White working class masculinity in the 1990s. In M. Fine, L. Weiss, L. C. Powell, & L. M. Wong (Eds.), *Off white: Readings on race, power, and society* (pp. 210–228). New York: Routledge.

Wellman, D. (1999). Transforming received categories: Discovering cross-border identities and other subversive activities. In C. Clark & J. O'Donnell (Eds.), *Becoming and unbecoming white: Owning and disowning a racial identity* (pp. 78–91). Westport, CT: Greenwood Press.

West, C. (1993a). The new cultural politics of difference. In C. McCarthy & W. Crichlow (Eds.), *Race, identity, and representation* (pp. 11–23). New York: Routledge.

West, C. (1993b). *Race matters.* Boston: Beacon.

West, C. (2004). *Democracy matters: Winning the fight against imperialism.* New York: The Penguin Press.

White, J. (1995, July 3). Forgive us our sins. *Time,* p. 29.

Wise, T. (2003, July 8). *White supremacy: No one is innocent.* Available at http://www.tolerance.org/news/article_tol.jsp?id=800

Williams, R. A. (1990). *The American Indian in Western legal thought: The discourses of conquest.* Oxford, UK: Oxford University Press.

Wulf, S. (1997, April 28). The lion and the tiger. *Time,* p. 86.

Yates, A. (1987). Current status and future directions of research on the American Indian child. *American Journal of Psychiatry, 144,* 1135–1142.

Zeichner, K. (1996a). Educating teachers for cultural diversity. In K. Ziechner, S. Melnick, & M. L. Gomez (Eds.) *Currents of reform in preservice teacher education* (pp. 133–175). New York: Teachers College Press.

Zeichner, K. (1996b). *Educating teachers for cultural states: An international review.* London: Falmer Press.

Zinn, H. (2003). *A people's history of the United States: 1942–present.* New York: HarperCollins.

Index

About the Author

Since his immersion as a young man in the civil rights revolution of the 1960s, **Gary R. Howard** has been working with colleagues throughout the United States and many other parts of the world to bring a healing vision to schools, universities, and other organizations. He travels extensively, speaking and providing workshops on diversity and social justice issues. He lives in Seattle, where he writes, plays with his three grandchildren, and serves as President and Founder of the REACH Center for Multicultural Education. Responses to this book and requests for information about his presentations can be addressed to him via email at *garyhoward@earthlink. net*. Information about the REACH Center is available at *www.reachctr.com*.